Princeton

A Picture Postcard History of Princeton and Princeton University

Nassau Hall, Princeton University, Princeton, N.J.

63843

by William K. Evans

Introduction by Leslie L. "Bud" Vivian, Jr.

ALMAR PRESS
BOOK PUBLISHERS

4105 Marietta Drive, Vestal NY 13850
(607) 722-0265 and 6251

DEDICATION

Dedicated
To The Memory
of

Frederic E. Fox
Class of 1939

Keeper of Princetoniana
Princeton University

He Was The Ultimate Expert
On Princeton Trivia

Library of Congress Cataloging-in-Publication Data

Evans, William K.
Princeton: A Picture Postcard History of Princeton and Princeton University/by William K. Evans. - 1st ed.
Introduction by Leslie L. Vivian, Jr.
     p. cm.
Includes bibliographical references and index
ISBN 0-930256-18-2
1.   Princeton (N.J.)—History—Pictorial works. 2. Princeton University—History—Pictorial works. 3. Postcards—New Jersey – Princeton. I. Title.
F144.P9E94 1992
974.9'65—dc20

                                                                                            92-24805
                                                                                            CIP

First Edition, First Printing   April 1993

PRINTED IN THE UNITED STATES OF AMERICA

Published by: Almar Press
                 4105 Marietta Drive
                 Vestal, New York 13850-4032

For a complete catalog of "A Picture Postcard History" Books covering many subjects and a variety of other publications contact the ALMAR PRESS, 4105 Marietta Drive, Vestal, New York 13850-4032. Telephone (607)722-0265 and 6251. Voice and FAX (607)722-0265.

PREFACE

Welcome to the world of Princeton through Deltiology, more commonly known as Postcard Collecting. Although picture postcards (and the inevitable collectors) were plentiful in Europe during the last decades of the 19th century, restrictive postal laws in the U.S.A. hampered the industry. At the end of the century, Congress loosened the restrictions and launched our country into the "Golden Age" of postcards. For the first time, private printers were permitted to publish and sell postcards to be mailed at the same rate as governmental Postal Cards. The rate was one cent instead of the two cents required for letters. The final step to achieve the picture postcard format as we know it today was taken in 1907 when permission was given to divide the back, or address side, into two parts; the message on the left and the address on the right. This change permits the collector to classify and date the postcards into "Divided Back" and "Undivided Back." Printers in the U.S.A. and Germany (where most of the postcards were produced) were able to provide the Postcards at a retail cost of one to two cents each. Therein an American tradition, a fad was born, and in 1908 approximately 678 million postcards were mailed in the U.S.A. This number could be divided into almost eight postcards for every man, woman, and child in the country. Postcards were avidly collected in albums for display on the parlor table. As the fad faded the albums were relegated to the attic where millions of the postcards were preserved for the edification and enjoyment of current collectors.

In preparing this book, an objective was to include only postcards from the 1910 to 1920 period which roughly coincides with the "Golden Age." The text includes many facts; however, they are leavened by bits of trivia which are the interesting footnotes to history and provide additional life to the subject. Although buildings are featured on the picture postcards they almost seem to have a life of their own. Over the years, they have been renamed, remodelled, recycled, restored, and relocated. We know that change is constant and as you read these words some of this text will be out of date.

These postcards show a small, peaceful, and apparently placid town; however, our era was one of change. The Turning Basin, on the Delaware and Raritan Canal, was a rough and ready commercial section of town; the author is unaware of any postcards that depict it. The College of New Jersey had recently adopted a new name, Princeton University and the new president, Woodrow Wilson, was installing his preceptorial system for intensive instruction in small groups. The monumental battle over the Graduate College was building up, the alumni were up in arms over the plan to ban eating clubs, and the dream of having a lake became a reality. In town, the new public high school had graduated its first class, the local water supply was assured by digging a well 490 feet deep, electric lights were replacing gas fixtures, and plans were being made to pave some of the streets. As one person said, "Princeton was a town with one foot still in the 19th century and one foot gingerly testing the 20th century."

As you examine the illustrations and text, please attempt to mentally reconstruct the turn-of-the-century context. Imagine the excitement of suddenly being able to send a lovely picture of your town to your aunt (who has never travelled more than 20 miles from her home). Remember that transportation was by train, trolley car, horse-drawn conveyance, bicycle, or on foot; automobiles were curiosities. Everyday communication was person-to-person or by mail; the telegraph was expensive, telephones were rare, and the radio-television age was an inventor's fantasy. An important point relative to postcards was that mail service was amazingly efficient. Princeton had three mail deliveries per day and mail to Maine (for example) was usually overnight.

One of the frustrations and delights of collecting postcards is that you can expect the unexpected. No one knows how many different postcards were produced. Unlike stamps and coins for which our government maintains detailed records of the quantities produced, we do not know how many manufacturers of postcards existed and what cards were published. As a disposable commercial product, the publishers gauged their markets according to the potential sales and as a result some buildings or other scenes were not memorialized on postcards. For example, Stanhope Hall and Joseph Henry House appear only as backdrops for other buildings and the Class of 1877 Laboratory (which stood near the present Firestone Library) never appeared on a postcard. Off campus, many of the beautiful homes, such as Guernsey Hall (on the Marquand Estate - now Marquand Park) were never published on postcards. In an era when trolley cars and fire engines were popular subjects for postcards, it is inexplicable that they are not known to be represented on Princeton postcards considering the fact that Princeton had two interurban trolley lines. For collectors there is always the hope that missing subjects will appear someday from their hiding places.

Although national and international firms published picture postcards of Princeton, special mention should be made of the local publishers. The earliest one was Richard Roland, Stationer, at 74 Nassau Street (Upper Pyne). Roland's clerk, William C. Sinclair, married Laura Rowland, and acquired the business. Later, he hired a local young man, Harold Hinkson, who eventually became the owner. The store remained on Upper Pyne until the building was razed in the 1960's and Hinkson continues to operate next door in the former home of the famous "Balt", the Baltimore Dairy Lunch. Local pharmacist, Joseph Priest's West End Drug Store, whose initials are preserved in the trim over the door of the Town Topics, Marsh & Co., (which suspended operation), and F.F. Chadwick all published a few postcards. The Van Marter name is frequently seen as a publisher; however, the most prolific publisher was Christie Whiteman, a legendary town barber, mail order entrepreneur, and licensed phonograph dealer. He recognized the market for postcards and followed the customary practice of purchasing postcards from large manufacturers with his name imprinted as the publisher. He also purchased a camera and published postcards from his own photographs.

For my fellow postcard collectors the text for each postcard lists pertinent data about the publisher, manufacturer, type of card, postmark (if mailed) and the value index. To explain the last category, it is useless to attempt to place a dollar value on a particular postcard. Such values are an educated guess at best and they quickly become out-of-date. The five classifications of values represent my subjective opinion based on almost twenty years of examining thousand of postcards in dealer's stocks and collections. Many factors enter into the value of a postcard. One example is a pertinent message written by the sender that classifies a particular postcard as "A—Very Rare" although the Postcard itself would be "E—Common." Other factors include the scene, postmark(s), stamps, condition of the Postcard, etc. The classifications are:

A - Very Rare
B - Rare
C - Scarce
D - Unusual
E - Common

Finally, I hope that readers of this book will enjoy it and will come away with a feeling for what Princeton was like in the first two feisty decades of this century.

William K. Evans

Princeton, New Jersey

—

ACKNOWLEDGEMENTS

I am indebted to so many resources that is risky to list any of them. Please note the Bibliography. Of the written sources, two volumes stand over all of the others. They are, of course, A PRINCETON COMPANION by the late Alexander Leitch and PRINCETON UNIVERSITY LAND 1752-1984 by Gerald Breese. Both are treasure troves of information about the town as well as the university. Both are easy to read as novels. Treasures were also mined from the Princeton Public Library, the Historical Society of Princeton, and the Seeley G. Mudd Manuscript Library, Princeton University.

Leading the list of individuals is my forbearing wife, Sis, who has helped me, discussed with me, and prodded me to complete the task. Alfred Weiner, my publisher, deserves a medal for putting up with me and Carolyn Weiner has my thanks for proposing the project. Thanks to Harvey N. Roehl for his careful reading of the text and suggestions for improvement. My Friend William K. Selden has supplied me with information in our conversations in addition to his books.

INTRODUCTION

Once upon a time . . . and not so very long ago, there were no post-cards!

Until the end of the last century, handwritten letters were the basic means of sending personal communications around the world. Family and friends had to rely on something more then the "Wish you were here" greeting which is so familiar to us today on the picture postcard. Travelers in the earlier days were challenged to develop their power for descriptive writing to convey pictures of landscapes, people, roads, canals, buildings, etc., not otherwise visible to the people back home.

Then, in 1873, the U.S. Government Postal Card appeared. Postal authorities authorized messages to be sent through the mail without an envelope. The address was on one side and the writing on the other side. No picture was allowed and the postage was one cent. Twenty years passed before the postal authorities agreed that a picture could be used in lieu of a written message. In 1898, private printers were autho-rized to publish postcards to be mailed at the same one cent rate as the government postal cards. The evolution to the format of today was completed in 1907 when the postal authorities permitted the back of the postcard to be divided into two parts – the left side for the message and the right side for the address.

This bit of history is important to an understanding of the time brackets within which today's Deltiologists must work. When these Postcard Collectors convene to buy or swap postcards relating to their special interest, they cannot hope to obtain any postcards earlier than the startup dates indicated above.

Had postcards come into being earlier, one can be assured that the author of this thoughtful and delightful compendium, Bill Evans, would have uncovered them. His curiosity about his hometown, its early history and its people, has led other Deltiologists to think of the Evans Family as "The people who collect Princeton." As a result, their personal effort to hunt down postcard evidence of Princeton's past has been nicely supplemented by self-appointed assistants, caught by their enthusiasm and appreciation.

This marvelous collection of old postcards, with its carefully arranged selection of places, people, and things, is testimo-ny to its success in taking us back a few generations and enhancing our understanding of Princeton as it is today in relation to the small college town of yesterday.

The magic mixture of campus and community achieved in this book reveals Bill's sensitivity to the diversity of interests that comprise a college town with a history dating back to 1696. The townspeople's invitation to the College of New Jersey (now Princeton University) to settle on the south side of Nassau Street in 1756 initiated some of the changes which subse-quently came to pass, as recorded herein.

For bringing this stimulating example of Deltiology-at-its-best to Princeton, New Jersey, in the waning years of the twen-tieth century, the Evans' deserve more than congratulations.

Thus, the reason for wanting to write this Introduction is to speak for tomorrow's readers as well as today's readers and to say for all of us:
>THANK YOU VERY MUCH:
>>Sincerely,
>>Leslie L. Vivian, Jr.
>>(Longtime friend and admirer)

N.B. When he retired from Princeton University, Mr. Vivian held the post of Director, Community and Regional Affairs; and Associate Secretary of Princeton University.

'BUD' VIVIAN, AMBASSADOR (RET.)

ABOUT THE AUTHOR

Bill Evans' introduction to Princeton was in 1935, when the University of Pennsylvania and Princeton University resumed their historic football relationship. Although the schools met in many other sports, the football rivalry had been suspended in 1894 following the bloody game familiarly termed "The Second Battle of Trenton." As a member of the University of Pennsylvania's marching Band, Bill made the trek for the games from Philadelphia to Princeton on the customary special train. After his graduation from the Wharton School in 1938. Bill moved from Philadelphia to Trenton to begin his accounting career. In 1941, he married Sis and their daughter was born a few years later. After World War II, they began to look for a permanent home and they searched for an established family community with good public schools. Princeton seemed to be the ideal answer; they moved here in 1951. Later, Bill left the industrial accounting field to join the administrative staff of the Princeton School System. He retired in 1982.

When they moved to Princeton, Bill and Sis became involved in school and church activities. As an Elder in the First Presbyterian Church, Bill was asked to serve on the Cemetery Committee and was soon conducting tours of the historic Princeton Cemetery. The dual 35 year involvement in local schools and a 250-year-old cemetery fanned his interest in local history. Since his retirement, Bill has delved further into the subject by giving local walking tours for the Historical Society of Princeton.

The evolution of Bill's interest in picture postcards follows a pattern duplicated among thousands of Deltiologists. As children, he and Sis had shoe boxes of postcards to examine on rainy days. Both came from families of frequent travellers, and postcards from all over the world found homes in those boxes. Somehow, the postcards survived childhood, the teen years, and adulthood; these postcards remain in their collection.

About twenty years ago, while browsing at an antique show, Bill found a dealer with a small stock of postcards for sale. In that batch he found an early postcard showing Princeton University's Nassau Hall, for which he happily squandered a quarter. Not long after that he discovered that the Washington Crossing Collectors Club met in nearby Titusville, New Jersey. A visit to a meeting sealed his fate as a postcard junkie.

It soon became apparent to him that to preserve his sanity it would be necessary to specialize in his collection. Therefore, he concentrated on the collecting of Princeton and its environs, as well as those for his alma mater, the University of Pennsylvania. Despite these limitations he has several thousand postcards in the collection. However, among collectors that is considered to be a modest number of postcards to have in a collection.

Bill enjoys sharing his postcards. He has shown slides of them to various groups including church, civic, senior citizen, and social. In addition, postcard clubs are always seeking programs as are nearby historical societies. The Historical Society of Princeton exhibited a portion of the collection for almost six months and 5,000 people visited it.

DIAGRAM OF THE PRINCETON CAMPUS

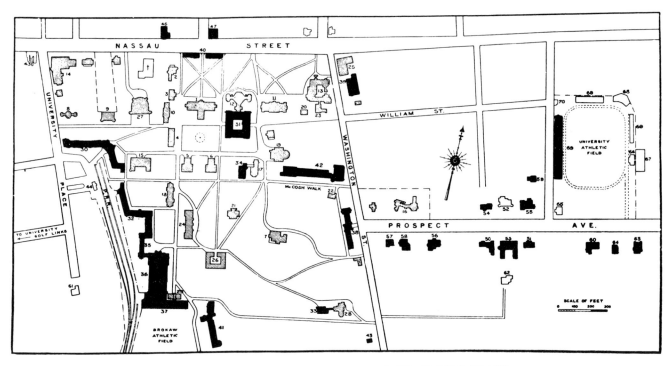

BUILDINGS ERECTED SINCE 1896 ARE INDICATED IN SOLID BLACK

1.	Nassau Hall	1756	24.	Albert B. Dod Hall	1890	46.	Upper Pyne Building	
2.	Dean's House	1756	25.	Chemical Laboratory	1891	47.	Lower Pyne Building	
3.	University Offices	1803	26.	David Brown Hall	1891	50.	Ivy Club	
4.	West College	1836	27.	Alexander Hall	1892	51.	Cap and Gown Club	
5.	Clio Hall	1838 and 1893	28.	Infirmary	1892	52.	Tiger Inn	
6.	Whig Hall	1838 and 1893	29.	Brokaw Memorial	1892	53.	Cottage Club	
7.	Prospect	1849				54.	Colonial Club	
8.	Halsted Observatory	1869	30.	Blair Hall	1897	55.	Elm Club	
9.	Old Gymnasium	1869	31.	University Library	1897	56.	Cannon Club	
10.	Reunion Hall	1870	32.	Stafford Little Hall	1899	57.	Campus Club	
11.	Dickinson Hall	1870	33.	Infirmary Annex	1899	58.	Quadrangle Club	
12.	Chancellor Green Library	1873	34.	Dodge Hall	1900	59.	Terrace Club	
13.	School of Science	1873	35.	Stafford Little Hall	1901	60.	Charter Club	
14.	University Hall	1876	36.	New Gymnasium	1903	61.	The Bachelors' Club	
15.	Witherspoon Hall	1877	37.	University Power Plant	1903	62.	Bayles Farm	
16.	Observatory of Instruction	1878	38.	Class of 1879 Dormitory	1904	63.	Tower Club	
17.	Murray Hall	1879	39.	Civil Engineer'g Laboratory	1904	64.	Key and Seal Club	
18.	Edwards Hall	1880	40.	Fitz Randolph Gateway	1905	65.	Osborn House	
19.	Marquand Chapel	1881	41.	Patton Hall	1906	66.	Field House	
20.	Biological Laboratory	1887	42.	McCosh Hall	1906	67.	Cage	
21.	Art Museum	1887	43.	Alumni Weekly Building		68.	Grand Stand	
22.	Magnetic Observatory	1889	44.	Railroad Station		69.	Open Stands	
23.	Dynamo Building	1889	45.	Diagnostic Station		70.	Thompson Gateway	

The Big Cannon depicted in this postcard was the larger of two field pieces abandoned by the British during the American Revolution. During the War of 1812, it was moved to New Brunswick as part of that city's defenses. In 1835, the Princeton Blues, a military company of local citizens, recovered it, but when their wagon broke down, it was abandoned on the outskirts of town. Several years later, a group of students from the College of New Jersey led by Leonard Jerome, grandfather of Winston Churchill, rescued it. In 1840, it was planted muzzle down in Cannon Green, where it remains today.

Christie Whiteman, the publisher of this postcard, was an energetic local entrepreneur. He was a town barber and also operated an active mail order business from the basement of his home. He was the first phonograph distributor in central New Jersey, and opened Princeton's first movie house. When the postcard craze hit, he became a prolific publisher of postcards for local consumption. This postcard is wholly a hometown creation. The artist, Charles La Tourette, was also the owner, publisher, and editor of The Princeton Packet, one of the oldest weekly newspapers in the country. Today, the paper continues to be published on a semi-weekly basis.

COPYRIGHT 1910. CHRISTIE WHITEMAN, PRINCETON, N. J.

Publisher: Christie Whiteman, Princeton, NJ * Manufacturer: Beckman & Co., Philadelphia, PA * Type: Colored, Divided Back * Postmark: Not Used * Value Index: C

Publisher: Not Indicated * Manufacturer: Not Indicated * Type: Divided Back * Postmark: April 16, 1908 * Value Index: A

Many of the early postcards were not merely printed and colored. Pictures of ladies sometimes had real hair and cloth glued on them. Other postcards were decorated with silk threads, tinsel, glitter, beads, feathers, lace, felt, fur, and ribbon. Still others had moving parts. These novelties always sold at a premium, but perhaps the most expensive were the "Hold To Lights." These postcards were made from laminated stock with an underlayer of translucent paper. The top layer was die-cut, which created the illusion of an illuminated night scene when it was held to the light. For example, a view of an office building would show the windows ablaze with light. It may sound prosaic today, but keep in mind that electric lighting was relatively new at the turn of the century.

The example shown had a cloth insert with the banner embroidered in the orange and black Princeton colors. The writer and the recipient obviously have Princeton as a common bond of friendship. Perhaps the two women remembered house parties at the University during the Gay 90's which inspired the message, "How the Orange and Black brings back old times to the mind."

1

Postcards using the Princeton University symbols; the orange and black colors and the tiger, have always been popular. They express the loyalty, school spirit, and pride which both town and gown have traditionally displayed for the institution. The combining of orange and black was accidental. Shortly after the end of the Civil War, orange ribbon badges were introduced; the printing of the badges was in black ink. In 1874, a student had a thousand yards of orange and black ribbon manufactured for a rowing regatta in Saratoga, New York, where they quickly sold out. The colors became standard for athletic uniforms and were celebrated in school songs.

At the sesquicentennial celebration in 1896, when the College of New Jersey was officially renamed Princeton University, Allen Marquand, Professor of Art and Archaeology, urged that the colors be changed to orange and blue. Part of his argument was that because Nassau Hall had been named in memory of King William III of the House of Nassau, it would be appropriate to adopt the orange and blue colors of the House of Nassau. Thirty years of tradition prevailed, and the trustees adopted orange and black as the official colors for academic gowns. This confirmed a faculty decision which had been made in 1868 at the request of the student body.

Copyright 1911
Christie Whiteman,
Princeton, N. J.

Publisher: Christie Whiteman, Princeton, NJ, * Manufacturer: G & S, NY "Photochrome" * Type: Colored, Divided Back * Postmark: Not Used * Value Index: B

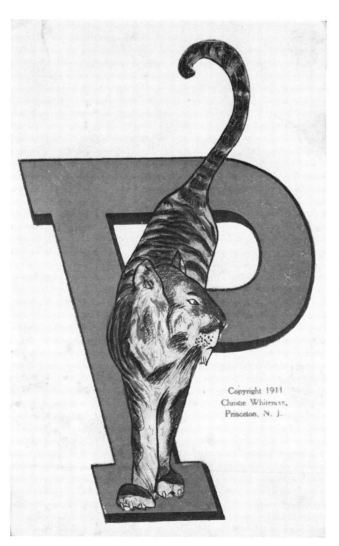

Copyright 1911
Christie Whiteman,
Princeton, N. J.

The message on the back of the postcard reads, "Just left the baseball game. Tigers beat the Bulldogs." In other words, Princeton beat Yale. As were the orange and black colors, the symbol of the tiger was also the subject of controversy. At graduation, Dr. Woodrow Wilson's class (1879) gave a pair of lions to guard the main entrance to Nassau Hall. In the ensuing debate of lion vs. tiger, the faculty favored the lion as a more regal symbol, but the students finally prevailed with the more popular symbol of the tiger. It not only fit the school colors, but songs and cheers of the day used the tiger as a theme. In 1911, when this postcard was issued, the Class of 1879 replaced the Nassau Hall lions with the existing pair of bronze tigers.

Publisher: Christie Whiteman, Princeton, NJ, Card No. E-6110 * Manufacturer: American News Co., NY, Leipzig, Berlin—"Photochrome" * Type: Colored, Divided Back * Postmark: June 18, 1921 * Value Index: B

Van Marter is a familiar name on local postcards. There were at least three members of the family who published postcards in competition with Christie Whiteman. In those days, when communication was always written, "The Tiger and Maid" must have been ideal for a student to write to his girl. If she participated in the postcard collecting passion of her time, she would place this nice drawing in her album to remind her of a special friend at Princeton.

Publisher: Van Marter * Manufacturer: Not Indicated * Type: Colored, Divided Back * Postmark: Not Used * Value Index: B

The erudite tiger with the quill pen conveys a subtle message. The unfinished "Princeton" under his paw seems to say, "Please Write." What young woman could resist that plea from a friend at an important university in a small central New Jersey college town?

Beyond the bare initials, "S. P. S.," — or were his initials "S. P. C.,"? — the artist is un-known. There are several local postcards drawn by him; he may have been a local person.

Publisher: Probably Van Marter * Manufacturer: Not Indicated * Type: Colored, Divided Back * Postmark: September 4, 1908 * Value Index: B

This postcard is printed in black ink on brown leather. Many nonpaper materials have been used in the manufacture of postcards—wood, birchbark, metal, and others. In the first decade of the 20th century, leather postcards were very popular. Frequently, they were imprinted with a brief moral or a visual joke. For example, a bull is butting a man over a fence, and the man says, "I will be over shortly." They often portrayed a lovely lady with her picture hat, wasp waist, and flowing gown. Of course, for college town consumption, she always waved an appropriate banner for the local school. The leather must have been a real novelty in its day. The postcard itself is the message as there is little room for writing a personal note.

Publisher: W. S. Heal * Manufacturer: W.S. Heal * Type: Leather, Undivided Back * Postmark: Not Used * Value Index: B

Publisher: Not Indicated * Manufacturer: Not Indicated * Type: Leather, Undivided Back * Postmark: October 26, 1906 * Value Index: C

Another leather postcard. This novelty material seems to have been especially popular around 1905. Judging by the narrow time frame of its use, it may have been banned by the postal authorities. The leather is very limp and flexible, and could have jammed the postal machinery.

The solid orange and black colors of the hat, dress, and banner were painted on the surface by hand. The design provided space for a message, and "Fred" added his somewhat ungrammatical embellishments when he sent it.

Apparently, a Princeton student mailed this from his hometown, Peoria, Illinois, to a nearby lady friend in Flanagan, Illinois.

Paintings of beautiful women have always been popular subjects for postcards, especially those published for the college trade. This lovely Queen of Clubs is from a four-card set titled, "College Queens"; there is a companion set of "College Kings." The schools represented on the eight postcards are Princeton, Columbia, Cornell, Harvard, Pennsylvania, and Yale from the present-day Ivy League, plus the Universities of Chicago and Michigan. The two midwest universities often appeared on the football schedules of the six eastern schools. According to aficionados of the sport, one of the great games of modern football was played between Princeton and heavily favored University of Chicago in 1922. After trailing badly in the early stages, Princeton fought back in the last twelve minutes to win by 21 to 18. It was the key game in Princeton's undefeated season.

The publisher of this rare postcard, Raphael Tuck & Sons, was a well-established British firm which proudly proclaimed its position as "Art Publishers to Their Majesties the King and Queen." When the postcard craze came along, it was a logical move for the company to enter this new market. In 1910, Raphael Tuck & Sons had over 15,000 postcard designs available.

Publisher: Raphael Tuck & Sons, London, England, "College Queens" Series, Card No.2767 * Manufacturer: Raphael Tuck & Sons, Chromographed in Berlin * Type: Colored, Divided Back * Postmark: Not Used * Value Index: A

Among collectors, "Signed Artist" postcards have always been in demand. Among the various examples shown in this book you will note that F. Earl Christy designed postcards for firms here and abroad. He was born in Philadelphia and learned his craft there. As one author put it, he "glorified, through the medium of the postcard, the rich college girl with her wispy-waisted gowns and fur muffs." The style of the drawings fits into the general category of the "Gibson Girls," a popular type of pinup in the early 1900s.

The publishers hired numerous artists to produce their vast varieties of postcards. Although many were undistinguished, there were also numerous ones with respected artistic reputations who devoted their efforts to postcards. The assumption is that postcard commissions were good bread-and-butter jobs between more prestigious assignments.

Publisher: American Postcard, Ullman Manufacturing Co., NY, Card No.1996, "College"* Series No. 93 * Manufacturer: Ullman Manufacturing Co., NY * Type: Colored, Divided Back * Postmark: Not Used * Value Index: B

This is another postcard drawn by F. Earl Christy. The early 20th century marked the beginning of womens' emancipation. In commenting on drawings of this genre, one author said, "The socialite Gibson Girl, who was taller than her mother, went to college, and played golf with male friends, gave a new look to the young woman,—." The 21-inch waist, made possible by tightly laced corsets, would soon disappear as women became active in areas which had been closed to them. The dress with the tiny waist was combined with broad shoulders, which served to emphasize the hips and bosom. With the flowing ankle-length skirts, the drawings were charmingly sexy.

The yell (cheer) printed on the postcard is a version of the "Locomotive," which was introduced in the 1890s. The words in the cheer start slowly and rhythmically and pick up speed, suggesting the sound of an old steam locomotive.

Publisher: Raphael Tuck & Sons, London, England, "University Girl" Series, Card No.* 2625 * Manufacturer: Raphael Tuck & Sons, London, England * Type: Colored, Divided Back * Postmark: Not Used * Value Index: B

This postcard by F. Earl Christy was drawn for a firm other than Raphael Tuck & Sons. A hallmark of his drawings is the veil, an outmoded item of dress which provided a certain aura of mystery to the wearer's features. It also had very practical uses. It helped to keep the lady's hat in place on her pompadour, whose soft roll of hair provided a rather unstable base. In addition to keeping her hat from blowing away when she rode in one of the early automobiles, which provided little or no protection, the veil protected the wearer from the wind, rain, and the dust of Princeton's unpaved streets and roads. The picture stands out on the card, because the heavy embossing raises the image of the girl away from the background, giving it a three-dimensional effect.

Publisher: EAS * Manufacturer: Made in Germany * Type: Embossed, Colored, Divided Back * Postmark: Not Used * Value Index: B

This picture of an animated young lady always seems to conjure up the same scene. Visualize the moment when she has arrived on a special football train at the Pennsylvania Railroad Station located at the Blair Tower steps. After picking him out of the festive crowd, she is running to her Princeton University boyfriend, who has come to meet her.

PRINCETON.

1516

Publisher: Ullman Manufacturing Co., NY, Card No. 1516 ∗ Manufacturer: Ullman Manufacturing Co., NY ∗ Type: Colored, Undivided Back ∗ Postmark: Not Used ∗ Value Index: C

College Girl Series 1   *Copyright, 1905, Souvenir Post Card Co., N. Y.*

Hurrah! Hurrah! Hurrah! Tiger! Sis! Boom! ah! Princeton!

The gift-wrapped football clearly indicates that the postcard was produced for the fall season. The picture was daring in its time—it actually displays a lady's calf! Also, the academic cap and gown were anachronistic; the Princeton University Coed did not appear until more than 60 years later.

It is interesting to note that the British version of the yell (cheer) on some of the other illustrations in this book differs from the American version. The Raphael Tuck & Sons postcards usually used "Hooray" in place of the more commonly used "Hurrah."

Publisher: Souvenir Post Card Co., NY, "College Girl" Series, Card No. 1 ∗ Manufacturer: Souvenir Post Card Co., NY ∗ Type: Colored, Divided Back ∗ Postmark: April 27, 1909 ∗ Value Index: B

Postcards in the "College Girl" genre customarily had a woman or a couple as the subject. Picturing the four happy young women hot-rodding down the road in their 1906 roadster results in an unusual postcard. In this era, not many women drove, especially without a male escort. Perhaps the young driver had picked up her friends at the Princeton Junction Station and was taking them, banners flying, to a football game at University Field.

Note that the automobile was steered from the right hand side. It also had a tiller rather than a steering wheel. Another prominent feature is the muff carried by one of the young women. It was a popular article of dress, because it not only kept her hands warm, but it also gave her something to do with her hands. A proper lady did not indiscriminately hold hands with her escort.

Publisher: Illustrated Post Card & Novelty Co., NY, Card No. 5006-11 * Manufacturer: Illustrated Post Card & Novelty Co., NY * Type: Colored, Undivided Back * Postmark: Not Used * Value Index: B

Hurrah! Hurrah! Hurrah!
Tiger! Sis! Boom! Ah! Princeton!

The drawing of a head and shoulders emphasizes the pennant, the stylish broad-brimmed hat, and the pompadour. The latter hair style, named after Madame Pompadour, was achieved by combing the hair "high over the forehead, either by drawing long hair over a roll, or by brushing short hair back so that it stands erect." This style can also be described as piling the hair on top of the head. As an important feature of high fashion, it is certain that the girlfriends of the Princeton students would follow it. In that era, football games were a showcase for the latest styles.

Note the same yell (cheer) as previously indicated. It was a generic yell with the American

Publisher: Douglass Post-Card Co., 27 North 10th Street, Philadelphia, PA * Manufacturer: Douglass Post-Card Co. * Type: Colored, Undivided Back * Postmark: Not Used * Value Index: B

"Hurrah" instead of the English "Hooray"; most of the schools had adopted some version of it.

It is certain that this illustration does not show the seal adopted by the trustees in 1896, when the College of New Jersey was renamed Princeton University. F. Earl Christy's revision to the design was probably aimed at the football season trade. The turtle neck sweater suggests cold weather, and he achieved the outdoor girl look by omitting the veil. Although the message and the July 1906 postmark do not completely support this theory, it is common to find seasonal postcards mailed at any time during the year.

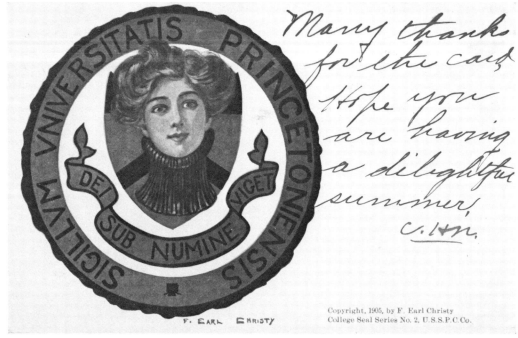

Publisher: U.S.S.P.C. Co., "College Seal" Series, Card No. 2, (Copyright 1905) * Manufacturer U.S.S.P.C. Co. * Type: Colored, Undivided Back * Postmark: July 20, 1906 * Value Index: B

There is no question that this was a football season postcard. These were frequently used between friends to report scores and gloat over victories. The message on the back of the postcard suggests that it was written by an alumnus in Trenton to a Yale friend in Belle Mead, New Jersey.

Although it was an English company, Raphael Tuck & Sons had a firm grasp of the American market. At the turn of the 20th century, most of the current Ivy League colleges were national powers in football. Although the American brand of this sport was unfamiliar to the English, Raphael Tuck & Sons featured football on many of its products aimed at the college trade. Note the use of "Hooray" instead of the American "Hurrah."

Publisher: Raphael Tuck & Sons, London, England, "Football," "Oilette," Card No. 2344 * Manufacturer: Raphael Tuck & Sons, London, England * Type: Colored, Undivided Back * Postmark: November 19, 1906 * Value Index: B

Football-related postcards were important to many colleges and universities as a method of communication, it is interesting to speculate on their special importance to an all-male student body isolated in a small central New Jersey town. This scene showing a couple sitting on the football was sent by a student in 1907 to his girl in Pottstown, Pennsylvania. The writer said, "Saturday is when we beat Amherst by a score of about 20-0, worse than the Indians. — Tonight I am going to hear Henry Van Dyke at the Y.M.C.A. on the `Holy Land'. — Wrestling now every day. Feeling fine. Weight still the same. Still busy as ever, but haven't forgotten you. A.F." The "Indians" undoubtedly referred to the team from the Carlisle (Pennsylvania) Indian School made famous by Jim Thorpe.

Publisher: Julius Bien & Co., NY, "College" Series No. 95, Card No. 954 (on face), (Copyright 1907) * Manufacturer: Julius Bien & Co., NY * Type: Colored, Divided Back * Postmark: November 7, 1907 * Value Index: B

During the heyday of postcards, many of those published were not really intended to be mailed; they were specifically designed for the collector. Sometimes, they came with their own mailing envelopes, despite the fact they conformed to the postcard format. Of course, they commanded a premium price.

This postcard is heavily embossed. During manufacture, the postcard was pressed between two special dies so that the design is raised in relief above the surface. Written by a mother to her daughter in Trenton, New Jersey, it must have been mailed in an envelope. The postcard has neither a stamp nor postmark, but it does have that perennial travel message, "Am doing Princeton today."

Note the protective shoulder and elbow pads worn by the football player. Presumably the young lady's mode of dress was appropriate for spending an afternoon in the chill of University Field at Prospect Avenue and Olden Street.

Ray, Ray, Ray, Tiger, Tiger, Tiger, Siss, Siss, Siss, Boom, Boom, Boom A-A-A-A-Ah, Princeton, Princeton, Princeton.

Publisher: Souvenir Post-Card Co., NY, "College" Series, Card No. 3, (Copyright 1907) * Manufacturer: Souvenir Post-Card Co., NY (Printed in Germany) * Type: Embossed, Colored, Divided Back * Postmark: Not Used * Value Index: B

At various times in our history, the Assunpink Indian Trail from Philadelphia, Trenton, and Lawrenceville was known as the King's Highway, Post Road, and Lincoln Highway. As it enters Princeton from the southwest, its prosaic name is Route 206; as you leave the bridge at the right side of the picture, it becomes Stockton Street.

The Stony Brook bridge was built in 1792 to replace one destroyed by order of General Washington after the Battle of Princeton. Comments in the press indicate that the State of New Jersey plans to build a modern, efficient, multilane poured-concrete bridge in place of this graceful structure.

This photographic postcard was printed about 1910, but it is

Publisher: Not Indicated * Manufacturer: Not Indicated * Type: Photograph (Azo) * Postmark: Not Used * Value Index: A

impossible to determine when the picture was taken. It appears, however, that the mill (upper left) was in operation. Worth's Mill, as it was known, predates the bridge by many years; it was built in 1715. Today we are reminded of it by a single remaining stone wall.

For you fishermen, please observe the natty fishing garb. Did you ever go fishing dressed in a three-piece suit, collar, tie, and straw skimmer? Also, did your equally well-dressed female companion sit peacefully on the bank, reading?

Not far from the Stony Brook Bridge is the Princeton Battlefield State Park, site of the January 3, 1777 battle which is considered a turning point in the Revolution. Following defeats on Long Island and the loss of New York City, General Washington was pushed across New Jersey by the British troops. National morale was low, and enlistments were running out. In an abrupt change, General Washington's surprise Christmas Eve victory at Trenton was quickly followed by the defeat and capture of the British troops at Princeton. These victories helped to restore the confidence of the colonies and the American troops.

This view of "Princeton's Battle Field" is where most of the fighting occurred. General Washington's

Princeton's Battle Field, Princeton, N. J.

Publisher: Edward J. Van Marter, Princeton, NJ, Card No. N.N. 2027/13, 8742 * Manufacturer: Printed in Germany * Type: Colored, Divided Back * Postmark: Not Used * Value Index: C

troops came over the ridge in the background and surprised the British. The land was the farm of Thomas Clarke, a member of one of the Quaker families who first settled Princeton. In 1770, he acquired 200 acres of land for his farm. Fortunately, this battlefield is one of the few to remain virtually unchanged in physical appearance since the Revolution. The original farmhouse still stands, and the foresight of local citizens and the State of New Jersey have minimized the encroachment of suburbia.

This postcard was published many years after the "Princeton's Battlefield" postcard. The pile of cannon balls has been embellished with an eagle. Both the eagle and the cannon balls have long since vanished. When asked about their disappearance, a local historian said, "They had to be removed, of course. They were of Civil War vintage."

When General Hugh Mercer of the Continental Army was wounded, he refused to be removed from the field and was laid by the oak tree which still stands at the center of the battlefield. He had been bayoneted seven times. The fighting moved on into the Village of Princeton, and General Mercer was taken to the nearby farmhouse of Thomas Clarke, where he died nine days later.

Monument marking spot where General Mercer fell in the Battle of Princeton, N. J.

Publisher: H. M. Hinkson, Stationer, Princeton, NJ * Manufacturer: The Albertype Co., Brooklyn, NY * Type: Black and White, Divided Back * Postmark: Not Used * Value Index: C

The terse misspelled legend on the postcard says "Monument erected in honor of General Hugh Mercer. House in background where he died."

The house wing visible to the right side in the picture is the original farmhouse in which Thomas Clarke lived with his brother and two sisters. Fortunately, the house survived the battle virtually unscathed. At least General Mercer had the best care available under the circumstances.

The house remained in the Clarke family until 1863, and has had only two subsequent owners, including the present one, the State of New Jersey. It has been part of Princeton Battlefield State Park since 1946. After restoration, the house was opened to the public on July 4, 1976, for the Bicentennial Celebration.

Monument erected in honor of Gel. Hugh Mercer House in background where he died.

Publisher: Van Marter, Card No. 2489/31 and 5419 * Manufacturer: Printed in Germany * Type: Colored, Divided Back * Postmark: Not Used * Value Index: D

The cannon no longer stands guard. Probably, as in the case of the pile of cannonballs, it was removed because it was a Civil War field piece.

Hale House, Princeton, N. J.   Where General Mercer died.

Publisher: W. C. Sinclair, Princeton, NJ, Card No. QA4715 ∗ Manufacturer: American News Co., NY, Leipzig, Dresden, Berlin, "Excelsior" (Made in Germany) ∗ Type: Black and White, Divided Back ∗ Postmark: Not Used ∗ Value Index: E

On the old postcards, the Clarke House was sometimes identified as "Hale House," and for good reason. The Clarke Family sold the house in 1863 to Henry E. Hale. Orphaned as a child, Hale was raised by the Bruere Family, who lived on the old Worth's Mill property. Fortunately for him, his parents left him a large inheritance which provided for his education and allowed him to enter his chosen profession. His early education was attained a private school in Freehold, New Jersey. He left Princeton in the fall of each year and did not return until the following spring. A 30-mile trip was not an easy journey before the Civil War.

When Hale matriculated at the College of New Jersey his ambition was to become a farmer. To this end, he apprenticed himself for two years to a Pennsylvania German farmer before purchasing the farm from the Clarke Family. He was a successful farmer and an outstanding leader in local church and civic activities. His son, also a Nassau Hall graduate, became a respected physician in New York City. On the death of his mother, he brought his family back to the Princeton farm. After World War II, the State of New Jersey exercised its power of eminent domain to form Princeton Battlefield State Park and more than 80 years of Hale Family residency came to an end.

The postcard clearly shows the post-Revolution additions to the Clarke farmhouse. The taller section at the right was the original building. At the time of the Battle of Princeton, the entrance was in what is now the rear of the house. The road which it faced was the one that General Washington used to reach Princeton when he marched his troops from Trenton. Only remnants of that road exist today.

This pastoral dirt road (circa 1910), less than a quarter of a mile long, is now a heavily traveled link between Stockton Street (Route 206) and Mercer Street (Princeton Pike). In the past, the street's name has been a source of complaint from local police. It seems that the street signs have been a coveted decoration for student rooms.

One side of the lane was the eastern border of Moses Taylor Pyne's estate, Drumthwacket, and the estate on the other side was Guernsey Hall, home of Professor Allen Marquand. After extensive subdividing, the remaining Drumthwacket property has passed into state ownership for use as a Governor's Mansion and center for state entertainment. Most of the Guernsey Hall property was left to the Borough of Princeton, and it is now known as Marquand Park. Guernsey Hall itself was preserved by being converted into several condominiums.

The name, "Lovers Lane," probably has a less romantic history than the words imply. After the Princeton and Kingston Turnpike opened in 1807, the little dirt road led to the home of the Loofburrow Family and thus became "Loofburrow's Lane." It is believed that the current name is an attractive corruption of a mundane original.

Lovers Lane, Princeton, N.J.

Publisher: Van Marter, Princeton, NJ, Card No. 2489/7 and 5395 * Manufacturer: Printed in Germany * Type: Colored, Divided Back * Postmark: April 16, 1912 * Value Index: C

In the scene shown on this postcard, you are standing near the intersection of Stockton and Mercer Streets. Today, the view on the right-hand side of the postcard would show the Battle Monument and Borough Hall. Also, you will not see a horse and buggy here anymore, especially one parked facing the wrong way. No doubt, there would be a long line of cars waiting for the traffic light to change.

The odd little island at the right is on Princeton Inn property near the drive that leads into the grounds. Its purpose seems to be for setting off the flag pole, which is barely noticeable in the picture. To the left of the island and in the left foreground, note the wrought iron hitching posts. Also, note that progress had reached Princeton; on the near side to the left of the buggy, the tall pole supports an electric street light. Bayard Lane stretches off to the right.

H 18355 Stockton Street, Princeton, N. J

Handcolored

Publisher: The Rotograph Co., New York City, NY, (Sol-Art Prints), Card No. H 18355 * Manufacturer: The Rotograph Co., New York City, NY (Printed in Germany) * Type: Colored, Undivided Back * Postmark: Not Used * Value Index: E

The original Princeton Inn, 1893-1918, was on the corner of Bayard Lane and Stockton Street. It passed into the hands of Miss Fine's School, a highly respected private school for girls. The school used the building until about 1965, when it joined with Princeton Country Day School to form the coeducational Princeton Day School. The new organization opened in its present location on the Great Road. After a complicated property exchange involving the Borough of Princeton and Princeton Theological Seminary, the old inn was razed to make way for the existing Borough Hall.

Those were the early days of the telephone. To call the Inn, you removed the receiver from the hook, placed it to your ear, waited for the operator to answer, and simply said, "8-A Princeton, please." The operator would then plug your line to the Inn's line on the switchboard and ring the called line. The unedited advertisement below is typed on the other side of the postcard.

Entrance and Lawns of Princeton Inn, Princeton, N. J.

Publisher: Not Indicated * Manufacturer: Not Indicated; possibly Detroit Photographic Co. * Type: Colored, White Bordered * Postmark: July 22, 1912 * Value Index: A

JUST A REMINDER
PRINCETON INN
Open all the Yearr
IDEAL SHORT RUN & STOPOVER
Lawns-Shady Trees-Tennis
MEALS AT ALL HOURS
Noted Cuisine-White Service
A LA CARTE
A College Inn
in a College Town

Under the aegis of Moses Taylor Pyne and others, the first Princeton Inn opened in 1893 and served the community and University until 1918. In 1897, it was in the headlines when the New York press attacked its liquor-serving policy as "Princeton's Official Saloon." The Presbyterian hierarchy became involved in the controversy, and the defense was led by Mr. Pyne. Nothing substantive seems to have resulted from the incident.

The grounds were spacious, as is indicated by the graceful curved driveway leading to the porte cochere at the main entrance. The stylish touring car must have been a real curiosity when this postcard was mailed on June 11, 1911. The baseball fan who wrote it said, "Came here by auto today to see the game. Had a dandy time. Won, and I feel good. Love to all. F. & E."

Princeton Inn, Princeton, N. J.

Publisher: The Rotograph Co., New York City, NY, Card No. 63416 * Manufacturer: The Rotograph Co., New York City, NY (Printed in Germany) * Type: Colored, Divided Back * Postmark: June 11, 1911 * Value Index: E

There has been little change to this view looking out Mercer Street toward the Princeton Theological Seminary and the Princeton Battlefield. Of course, the street has been paved and the right-hand curb is now lined with parking meters. Mercer Street, from Nassau Street to the Stony Brook, is the Princeton segment of the old turnpike, which is the most direct route to the City of Trenton. It is a main artery funneling traffic into Princeton; you will never see the street this empty of vehicles and people.

Close examination reveals, a square block of stone at the curb in front of each house. They were placed there as a step for dismounting from a horse-drawn vehicle.

Mercer Street, Princeton, N. J.

Publisher: Van Marter, Princeton, NJ, Card No. AA4271 * Manufacturer: American News Co., NY, Leipzig, Dresden, Berlin, "Excelsior" (Made in Germany) * Type: Sepia, Divided Back * Postmark: Not Used * Value Index: E

The third street to join Mercer and Stockton Streets at Nassau Street is Bayard Lane (part of Route 206). It was named for Samuel Bayard, valedictorian of the Class of 1784. He was a respected lawyer, who served the College of New Jersey as librarian, trustee, and treasurer. He was also the first Mayor of Princeton Borough and a founder and trustee of the Princeton Theological Seminary.

When this postcard was published (circa 1908), Bayard Lane led to the rural suburb of Princeton Township. It was lined with estates on the east and large homes on the west. At the Nassau Street corner, the first estate was the home of Edgar Palmer, University trustee and benefactor, followed by the homes of Colonel William Libbey, Professor of

Bayard Lane, Princeton, N. J.

Publisher: W. C. Sinclair, Princeton, NJ, Card No. B3137 * Manufacturer: American News Co., NY, Leipzig, Dresden, Berlin, "Excelsior" (Made in Germany) * Type: Black and White, Divided Back * Postmark: Not Used * Value Index: E

Physical Geography, and the Reverend Dr. Henry van Dyke, author, lecturer, Professor of English, and diplomat. Farther out was Merwick, where Dean Alexander Fleming West was establishing the embryonic Graduate School for Princeton University. On the west side are at least two homes which were moved from Nassau Street near University Place in 1878 to make room for the University Hotel (razed in 1916). One of them, which has been a hostelry known as Peacock Inn since 1902, was the 18th century home of Jonathan Deare, prominent Princeton lawyer and member of the New Jersey Provincial Congress during the Revolution.

Near the intersection of Bayard Lane, Stockton Street, and Mercer Street, University Place (once called Railroad Avenue) begins at Nassau Street. As you look down the hill toward the Pennsylvania Railroad Station, you can see at least three buggies on the dusty street. Until women matriculated in 1969, this thoroughfare was the western boundary of the undergraduate campus. University Hall, at the left, was torn down to be replaced by Madison Hall. The view along the right side of the street is virtually the same today. The house with the Gothic arch at the entrance is where F. Scott Fitzgerald roomed when he was enrolled at the University.

University Place, Princeton, N. J.

Publisher: W. C. Sinclair, Princeton, NJ, Card No. B3139 * Manufacturer: American News Co., NY, Leipzig, Dresden, Berlin, "Excelsior" (Made in Germany) * Type: Black and White, Divided Back * Postmark: Not Used * Value Index: E

Although this house has been enlarged, it continues to be located at 19 University Place. In 1905, it was privately owned and was undoubtedly leased by the Class of 1885 for the Reunion Weekend. Princeton University has owned the house since 1932, and it is now divided into several apartments.

The landmarks cited on the postcard disappeared many years ago. The railroad station was relocated approximately two city blocks away at its present location, and Halstead Observatory was torn down to make way for a dormitory.

If we consider the fact that 108 Baccalaureate Degrees were granted in 1885, then, for the 20th Class Reunion, we can assume that each survivor received one postcard. Also assuming that 100 postcards were printed for the reunion, how many of these photographs might have survived the intervening 87 years, and be available today?

HEADQUARTERS FOR PRINCETON '85 REUNION June 10-14 1905

The house is 19 University Place, 150 yds. from the Railroad Station, and opposite to the Observatory

Publisher: Princeton University Class of 1885 * Manufacturer: Not Indicated * Type: Photograph * Postmark: April 8, 1905 * Value Index: A

Initially, the railroad ran along the Delaware and Raritan Canal. In 1865, after the main line was moved south of U.S. 1, a connecting line between Princeton Junction and Princeton was constructed. It is familiarly known as "The Dinky" or the "P.J. & B." (Princeton Junction and Back).

As shown, the tracks once extended to the foot of the Blair Hall steps. The tower is the center section of Blair Hall, the first of the Collegiate Gothic dormitories built by Princeton University. The older building at the upper right is Witherspoon Hall (1877), once considered to be the most beautiful and luxurious dormitory in this country. It also had the distinction of being the first Princeton University dormitory to enjoy indoor plumbing.

Note the message Rob wrote to his girl friend, Gussie. Automobiles were a novelty in 1907.

Publisher: E.J. Van Marter, Princeton, NJ * Manufacturer: Printed in Germany * Type: Colored, Undivided Back * Postmark: January 15, 1907 * Value Index: C

This view of the railroad station shows Stafford Little Hall at the left. Continuing from the end of Blair Hill, Stafford Little Hall was the second of the Collegiate Gothic dormitories which soon dominated the western end of the campus. This style of architecture was the standard for the next half-century of building by Princeton University. Stafford Little Hall was built in two parts (1899 and 1901) along the uneven boundary between the campus and the railroad right-of-way. The boundary's twisted dogleg contour led F. Scott Fitzgerald to describe it as a snake winding its way from Blair Hall to the Gymnasium.

The double tracks and the horse-drawn vehicles indicate the time period of the scene, probably 1902. Also, the well-stocked newsstand testifies that the station was a busy place.

Publisher: Not Indicated, Card No. 63845 * Manufacturer: Not Indicated * Type: Colored, Divided Back * Postmark: Not Used * Value Index: C

Pennsylvania Railroad Station, Princeton, N. J.

Publisher: W. C. Sinclair, Princeton, NJ, Card No. B3141 * Manufacturer: American News Co., NY, Leipzig, Dresden, Berlin, "Excelsior" (Made in Germany) * Type: Black and White, Divided Back * Postmark: Not Used * Value Index: A

This postcard is probably the oldest picture among the three illustrations of the railroad station shown in this book. The scene also shows the buildings on University Place. The dominant four-story Hill Dormitory at 48 University Place continues in use today as the home of the "Daily Princetonian," the campus newspaper. Now it is squeezed in between Lockhart and Foulke Halls, dormitories erected in the 1920s.

The station, Princeton's third, has a special little niche in history. In 1903, on its way to Boston, the Liberty Bell was detoured into Princeton for public exhibit. The time schedule for display was 15 minutes! In 1913, the town shut down so the residents and students could see Woodrow Wilson off to his first inauguration. For years, a familiar sight at the station was Moses Taylor Pyne's private one-car train waiting for him to entrain for New York City.

The four tracks were later reduced to two. In 1917, the station was razed and a new one was built at the foot of the hill. Originally, there were extensive railroad sidings for commercial shipping needs and to accommodate special trains for football games. Now, they have been reduced to a single track to Princeton Junction.

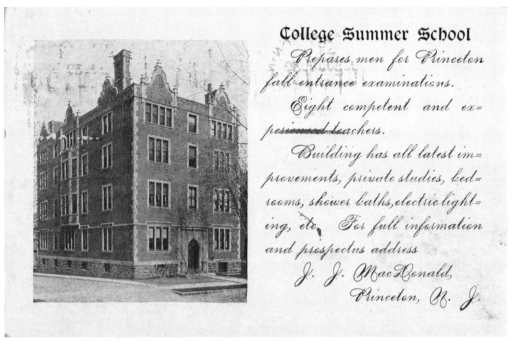

College Summer School

Prepares men for Princeton fall entrance examinations.

Eight competent and ex-perienced teachers.

Building has all latest im-provements, private studies, bed-rooms, shower baths, electric light-ing, etc. For full information and prospectus address

J. J. MacDonald,
Princeton, N. J.

Publisher: Privately published by J. J. MacDonald * Manufacturer: Not Indicated * Type: Black and White, Undivided Back * Postmark: July 30, 1907 * Value Index: A

Until the 1920s, Number 48 was unquestionably the most imposing structure on University Place south of Blair Hall. Built as a private dormitory, the property completed Princeton University's ownership along the east side of the street when it was acquired in 1949. Once known as Hill Dormitory, it is now simply called 48 University Place and houses the student newspaper, the "Daily Princetonian." Although the stone trim helps it to blend with its new neighbors, the brick building looks a bit out of place in an almost uniform row of stone buildings.

The architect who surveyed this building in 1980 for the Princeton Joint Historic Sites Commission was less than enthusiastic about it. He commented that it is "—BLAND— perhaps the most undistinguished building on campus."

From the amenities listed on this 1907 Postcard, it must have provided luxurious living accommodations.

The picture for this photographic postcard (circa World War I) was taken from the top of Holder Tower, part of a then relatively new dormitory complex. Nassau Street sharply divides the densely built-up village from the tree-shadowed campus of Princeton University. The buildings are concentrated along this historic thoroughfare; they thin out rapidly towards the open country. The farmland in the distance (rear of the photograph) yielded to suburbia in the post-World Ward II housing boom.

Just above the word "Princeton," is a building with a second floor balcony overlooking Nassau Street. This location was the entrance to the old Nassau Inn, where rooms extended for several buildings over the shops facing the street. This hostelry traces its history back to pre-Revolutionary times, when it was one of the numerous taverns serving the coach trade between Philadelphia and New York. The clutter of buildings behind the Inn housed many of the community's services, such as livery stables.

Publisher: Not Indicated * Manufacturer: Not Indicated * Type: Photograph (Azo) * Postmark: Not Used * Value Index: C

Further up the street, there is a black automobile parked, facing the wrong way, next to a utility pole. The Nassau Inn and all of the other structures to that point, plus all of the buildings in back of the inn were either razed or moved in the 1930s to make way for the Palmer Square complex.

This is an early turn-of-the-century photograph looking east from the head of Nassau Street. The curved curbing at the right marks the beginning of Mercer Street. The clapboard house behind the gas street light and the hitching posts stood approximately where Nassau Street Park now provides a bit of green space for downtown Princeton. The house with the steps on the other side of the street (left side of the photograph) continues to look approximately the same today. When Woodrow Wilson was President of the United States, he voted from his nearby brother-in-law's apartment.

NASSAU ST., PRINCETON, N.J.

Publisher: The Temme Co., Orange, NJ, (F.G.T. Co. Series), Card No. 2065 * Manufacturer: Made in Germany * Type: Colored, Divided Back * Postmark: Not Used * Value Index: D

The scene on this postcard can be closely dated. The tower which dominates Nassau Street was completed in 1910, and the postcard was mailed in 1913. Although many of the old postcards call it "Sage Tower," other records refer to it by its current name, "Holder Tower." Holder Hall and Holder Tower were given to the University by the widow of the financier, Russell Sage. It was named for one of her ancestors, a 17th century Quaker.

While it is clear that automobiles had arrived in Princeton, the eight or nine horse-drawn vehicles attest that they were not common. The small sign at the foot of the "Fireproof Garage" sign informs the public that it provides "Gasoline and Oil Here."

The clapboard house at the right

Nassau Street, showing Sage Tower, Princeton University.

Publisher: Van Marter, Princeton, NJ * Manufacturer: H. Wessler * Type: Black and Sepia, Divided Back * Postmark: September 20, 1913 * Value Index: D

has a sign that advertises "Upholstering." Just beyond it, on the other side of University Place, you can see the porch arches of University Hall, which would soon be demolished.

The Nassau Inn, Princeton, N. J.
J. B. Renwick, Proprietor

Publisher: J. B. Renwick, Card No. 1 (A491) * Manufacturer: Made in Germany * Type: Black and White, Divided Back
Postmark: Not Used * Value Index: C

This view of the Nassau Inn is an early one, probably taken about 1900. As indicated elsewhere, the Inn's rooms extended across the upper floors of all of the buildings shown. Advertising was more modest then; the only identifications are the small "Nassau Inn" sign on the tree and "Nassau Inn Stables" stretched across the alley. Obviously, the motor era had not yet begun. The sidewalk display in wooden crates indicates a food store; could this be the same "Joseph S. Hoff Meats & Vegetables Nassau Block" identified on another postcard.

The buildings shown are most of those on the Nassau Street edge of the area that was razed to permit the construction of Palmer Square. Down the alley on the left, all of the visible structures also

disappeared in the renewal project.

In the early days of postcards, it was rather unusual to have people in the scene. Here, among the twenty individuals watching the photographer at work, only one is female; even the two children are boys. A common feature on the postcards was to add a flag or flags to the original photograph; you will notice them on many of the illustrations in this book. The craftsmanship was usually shoddy and out of proportion. If you compare this flag and its pole to the height of the building, it would have been enormous.

Considered to be an outstanding example of Dutch Colonial architecture, the old Princeton Bank and Trust Company Building (1896) was modeled after the 16th century meat market of Haarlem in the Netherlands. The forerunner of this institution, the Princeton Banking Company, was located just a few doors to the west in an 1836 Steadman building which also housed the head cashier. In the 1960s, the bank moved into much larger quarters located in an addition to the Palmer Square complex. More recently, it was swallowed up in the national wave of financial mergers, but its trust division has retained at least some of its local identity, Princeton Bank and Trust Company, NA.

The oldest local bank, the Princeton Banking Company, was founded in 1834 when the town was on a crest of prosperity and expansion. The use of stagecoaches was at its zenith—the inns catered to 30 coaches per day, and as many as 100 horses were kept ready to supply teams. The Delaware and Raritan Canal Company was digging its way from Bordentown to New Brunswick, and its associate company, the Camden and Amboy Railroad and Transportation Company was building a railroad line from Bordentown to South Amboy. The town was growing and prospering and the new bank provided the needed capital.

PRINCETON BANK, PRINCETON, N. J.

Pub. by Edw. G. van Marter

Publisher: Edw. G. van Marter * Manufacturer: Made in Germany * Type: Colored, Divided Back * Postmark: Not Used * Value Index: E

This view from the head of Nassau Street, postmarked 1919, illustrates the dramatic changes which had taken place in approximately a single decade. The mini-park has been created to set off the new Battle Monument, soon to be dedicated; University Hall has given way to the new Madison Hall (built in 1916). Madison Hall is visible between the two trees framing Holder Tower; and Priest's Drug Store is seen at the right, where the offices of Town Topics are now located. The first house at the left is unchanged. As an indication of the future, automobiles have begun to take over the newly paved streets of downtown Princeton. Except for the increase in automobile traffic and for minor physical changes, a similar picture could be taken today.

Nassau Street Park, Holder Tower in distance.   Princeton, N. J.

Publisher: W. C. Sinclair, Princeton, NJ * Manufacturer: The Albertype Co., Brooklyn, NY * Type: * Postmark: January 1, 1919 * Value Index: D

This picture (circa 1910) was taken at the center of town, approximately in front of where the 1988 addition to the Nassau Presbyterian Church stands. In the distance is the five-story First National Bank building at the corner of Witherspoon Street. The historic Nassau Inn dominates the scene in the foreground. The entrance was below the balcony between the two trees at the left, and the rooms, extending down the block, were located over the shops on the street level. The guests had to watch their step, because the hall floors were at different levels as they progressed from building to building.

Note that the principal sign for the inn is on the facade of the second building. Two smaller signs are hung on the trunk of the tree in front of the entrance. The

Nassau Street, Princeton, N. J.

Publisher: W. C. Sinclair, Princeton, NJ, Card No. A4718 * Manufacturer: American News Co., NY, Leipzig, Dresden, Berlin, "Excelsior" (Made in Germany) * Type: Black and White, Divided Back * Postmark: Not Used * Value Index: C

upper one says, "Garage-Rear-Nassau Inn," and the lower one simply announces, "Nassau Inn." Motor vehicles had become a factor in the hotel business. Although hard to discern, by the trunk of the same tree is a two-chair shoeshine stand. At the curb nearby is an open vehicle—an early truck. All of the other conveyances are horse-drawn. The wagon backed up to the curb announces "Joseph S. Hoff Meats and Vegetables Nassau Block." The term "Nassau Block" has disappeared; it can only be assumed that it refers to the section of shops below the rooms of the Nassau Inn.

As part of one of the town's major hostelries, this dining room seems rather modest and unassuming. Hats and coats were hung on wall racks, and the decor was rather austere. However, opulence shows up in the table settings. On the heavy linen table covers, there are seven-piece silver place settings with large linen dinner napkins. Each table has its own glass water carafe, and an elaborate array of condiments.

Although the chandeliers are electric, the wall lights may have been fueled by gas. In the early days of using electricity, it was common to have both forms of lighting. Were the people suspicious of the new-fangled source of light and power?

John B. Renwick was the proprietor and operated the Nassau Inn

NASSAU INN, PRINCETON N J
JOHN B RENWICK PROP

Publisher: Leo Mayer, Office 32 Pomp Bldg., Easton, PA, Card No. R-48214 * Manufacturer: Leo Mayer, Easton, PA (Made in U.S.A.) * Type: Colored, Divided Back * Postmark: September 12, 1914 * Value Index: A

for many years. Later, he opened the restaurant, "Renwick's." His original establishment was in one of the stores beneath the Inn rooms, and the restaurant survived the upheaval of the Palmer Square development. It was a popular place to eat until it went out of business in the late 1960s or early 1970s.

In this illustration we have moved a half-block east from the Nassau Inn scene. The timbered building was Upper Pyne; its twin was Lower Pyne, which can be seen to the right on the far corner of Witherspoon Street. These two dormitories were built by Moses Taylor Pyne and were given by him to Princeton University. Mr. Pyne was a major benefactor of Princeton, and his name appears frequently in these descriptions. Each dormitory accommodated approximately 20 students, and in 1940, a comment was made, "Rooms in these dormitories, with their window-seats overlooking Nassau Street, are great favorites with upper classmen."

Nassau St., Princeton, N. J.

The tall building at the corner was the First National Bank, which was only three bays wide.

Publisher: Illustrated Postal Card Co., New York-Germany, Card No. 99.-9 * Manufacturer: Illustrated Postal Card Co., New York-Germany * Type: Colored, Undivided Back * Postmark: Not Used * Value Index: E

Only a few years after it was built, the neighboring building was razed so three more bays could be added. The craftsmanship was superb; today, you cannot tell where the addition meets the original.

This is a Nassau Street scene, but you are now looking from east to west. At the left, it appears that the FitzRandolph Gate at the entrance to the college campus has not yet been erected, therefore, the date of this Postcard is prior to 1905. Except for the utility poles, awnings, horse and buggy, and general lack of traffic, this particular vista is virtually the same today. On the far corner of Witherspoon Street stands the bulky First National Bank Building. Of course, it had not yet been expanded from three to six bays, and it still had the little stone balconies, which have been removed in recent years. Presumably, they were unsafe and a threat to the pedestrians walking below. Lower Pyne (in the right foreground) looks the same

Nassau Street, Princeton, N. J.

Publisher: Richard Rowland, Princeton, NJ, Card No. 165 * Manufacturer: National Art View Co., NY (Germany) * Type: Black and White, Divided Back * Postmark: Not Used * Value Index: C

today, although it has not been a dormitory for many years. The community is fortunate that the new owners have restored it to its original beauty and maintain the authentic features.

At the lower right, there is a busy shoeshine stand. This one is embellished with a large beach umbrella, probably in the orange and black university colors. Note how the bicycles are parked on the curb. Can you imagine anyone casually parking an unlocked bicycle in this way in the 1990s?

From the previous scenes of Nassau Street, we move ahead approximately fifteen years. The FitzRandolph Gate is visible at the right, the utility poles are gone, the First National Bank Building now has six bays, and the automobile has begun to replace the horse.

This Postcard was postmarked in Princeton on November 11, 1918, the first Armistice Day, now Veteran's Day. "Walter," the sender, must have been in a military training program at Princeton University. The quotation below is the message he sent to his mother in St. Louis, Missouri. Note the relief he expresses in the first sentence and the heartfelt longing in the last.

"Well, it has happened at last. Hurrah, hurrah. We were on parade this afternoon down this street - our main street. Was at Philadelphia Saturday and Sunday and the place was alive with flags. I suppose there were some great times there. The people in Philadelphia and New York went wild. Let's hope we'll all be home soon."

Nassau Street.   Princeton N. J.

Publisher: W. C. Sinclair, Princeton, NJ * Manufacturer: The Albertype Co., Brooklyn, NY * Type: Black and White, Divided Back * Postmark: November 11, 1918 * Value Index: A

The two-story wing of Upper Pyne, with the alley cut through, was the last building at the east end of Nassau Street razed in the 1930s for the construction of Palmer Square. The jeweler whose business was advertised over the rolled awning was Mr. Myron LaVake. The corporate descendant of this store continues to operate today on Nassau Street under the name of LaVake, Jewelers and Silversmiths. The remainder of Upper Pyne was destroyed in 1967 to make way for the addition to Palmer Square which houses the Chemical Bank - New Jersey.

Moses Taylor Pyne, Class of 1877, was a trustee of Princeton University and Chairman of the Committee on Grounds and Buildings. Pyne favored the timber and stucco construction of Tudor architecture. He built Upper and Lower Pyne and gave them to Princeton University. The ground floors were devoted to commercial enterprises, and the upper floors were dormitories for the students.

Publisher: Not Indicated * Manufacturer: Not Indicated * Type: Photograph (EKC), Divided Back * Postmark: Not Used * Value Index: C

Lower Pyne looks much the same today as when this picture was taken circa 1910. Considering the present-day U.S. mail service, it is interesting to note that in the early part of the century, Princeton had three daily mail deliveries. When Palmer Square was built, the Post Office moved to its current location. Until less than ten years ago, it served as the main regional post office. Later occupants of Lower Pyne were the Western Union Telegraph office and the Suburban Bus Company station.

Looking down Witherspoon Street, the sign which stretches over the sidewalk advertises the restaurant operated by Laurent Dupraz. Formerly a small hotel, the building continues to be used for food service; it is Lahiere's Restaurant.

The tree at the corner was used

Publisher: Van Marter, Princeton, NJ, Card No. 2489/33; 5421 * Manufacturer: Printed in Germany * Type: Colored, Divided Back * Postmark: Not Used * Value Index: D

to post notices and advertisements. It grew to an imposing size and eventually died, however, the location continues to be used for community announcements. The sign boards tend to overwhelm the sapling which has been planted; normal growth soon remedied the problem.

Although the fourth floor of the first building on the right served as the Masonic Temple for a total of 26 years, the structure was generally known as the Bickford Building. Princeton Lodge No. 38, F. & A. M., leased the space from 1914 to 1930. When the owner raised the rent, the lodge moved to Thomson Hall, which also housed the Princeton Borough offices. Apparently, the depression had a severe effect on the owners of the building, because in 1940, the fraternal group was lured back by the offer of a very attractive rent. It was the Masonic Temple until 1950. Shortly thereafter, the building was razed to be replaced by the F. W. Woolworth store which was in business at the time of this writing. Note the old-fashioned

Publisher: W. C. Sinclair, Princeton, NJ * Manufacturer: The Albertype Co., Brooklyn, NY * Type: Black and White, Divided Back * Postmark: Not Used * Value Index: C

gasoline pump at the curb in the lower right corner of the photograph.

This postcard is the only one in the author's collection which shows a commercial building not located on Nassau Street. As the sign proudly states, it was the Branch Building erected in 1909 on the southeast corner of Witherspoon Street and Spring Street, formerly Spring Garden Street. It replaced one of three buildings which had been destroyed in a spectacular fire. Renamed the Benson Building after World War II, it was burned to the ground in 1977 by the town's worst fire in several decades. The handsome replacement is known as the Henderson Building, and houses stores, offices, and apartments.

Publisher: Rex Post Card Co., 96 Warren St., NY, Card No. 405164m * Manufacturer: Printed in Germany * Type: Black and White, Divided Back * Postmark: September 21, 1914 * Value Index: A

Reading the front window of the corner store, it shows it to be the Princeton Confectionary & Ice Cream Company. The sidewalk sign, "Cinco," shows that they also sold cigars. A puzzling sign running beneath the plate glass advertises "Yellowstone Park —"; what could that have been? The company must have been fairly large, because the smaller building in the rear proclaims "Wholesale and Retail Ice C(ream)."

According to some of our senior residents, the basement was a large room with a concrete floor. It may have been one of the early movie theaters, and it had also been used as a roller skating rink. Dances were held on the third floor. The site must have been a good business location, because one of the trolley lines to Trenton terminated near the front door of this store.

The caption on this postcard is incorrect. Although Presidents' Row was established by the College of New Jersey, Princeton Cemetery has been owned and operated by the Nassau Presbyterian Church and its predecessors for over 200 years. In 1903, the headstones were in obvious disrepair; Princeton University has repaired and restored them. In the foreground, the headstone of the famous (or infamous) Aaron Burr, Jr., clearly shows chipping from souvenir hunters. Fortunately, the desire to own pieces of this particular rock has disappeared. Damage today is limited to natural causes. The wrought iron fence which can be seen behind the box graves apparently enclosed the area containing many graves of the Stocktons, one of the Quaker

Publisher: Detroit Photographic Co., Detroit, MI, Card No. 7268 * Manufacturer: Detroit Photographic Co., Detroit, MI * Type: White Border, Colored, Undivided Back * Postmark: Not Used * Value Index: D

families who founded Princeton. One grave is that of Commodore Stockton, grandson of the signer of the Declaration of Independence, naval hero, twice conqueror of Los Angeles in the Mexican War, a diplomat who laid the groundwork for the founding of Liberia, and a driving force for the building of the Delaware & Raritan Canal. Many believe that he was a more colorful figure than Aaron Burr, Jr., although he certainly never caught the public imagination to the same degree.

The College of New Jersey acquired the original burial ground in 1757, one year after it moved to Princeton. In 1783, the Presbyterian Church exchanged land adjoining the church building adjacent to the college for the burial ground in the country, with the added commitment that there would be no burials next to the church. Obviously, the college did not appreciate the idea of having a cemetery practically on its front lawn.

The postcard shows the Presidents' Plot, where all except four of the deceased presidents of Princeton University are interred. Jonathan Dickinson (1746-1747) is buried in Elizabeth, New Jersey, Samuel Finley (1761-1766) in Philadelphia, Pennsylvania, Francis Landey Patton (1888-1902) in Bermuda, and Woodrow Wilson

Publisher: Van Marter, Princeton, NJ, Card No. 2489/28, 5416 * Manufacturer: Printed in Germany * Type: Colored, Divided Back * Postmark: Not Used * Value Index: C

(1902-1910) in Washington, DC. In 1878, John Frelinghaysen Hageman, Princeton historian, referred to the cemetery as "The Westminster Abbey of America." The list of individuals buried here include world-famous theologians from the Princeton Theological Seminary, the parents of Paul Robeson, Paul Tulane (of Tulane University fame), and Henry van Dyke (preacher, professor, author, poet, and diplomat).

Princeton Cemetery has been enlarged several times through mergers and gifts of land and it consists of approximately twenty acres. A common assumption is that it is filled. This is an easy mistake to make, because only the older, historic section is visible from the street.

Whether Aaron Burr, Jr., was villain or hero is still hotly debated. The Aaron Burr Association is devoted to clearing his name of what it considers unfounded and unjust libels. The unassuming headstone on his grave succinctly tells the highpoints in his life:

Aaron Burr
Born February 6, 1756
Died September 14, 1836
A Colonel in the Army of the Revolution
Vice President of the United States
from 1801 to 1805

A persistent myth is that he was buried "in the dark of night" so that the college students would not riot. Actually, the president of the college led a service in Nassau Hall, and the funeral cortege accompanied the

Graves of Aaron Burr & Jonathan Edwards, Princeton, N.J.

Publisher: H. C. Leighton Co., Portland, ME * Manufacturer: Made in Germany * Type: Colored, Undivided Back * Postmark: Not Used * Value Index: D

body to Princeton Cemetery, where he was buried with full military honors. An interesting footnote demonstrates the public's fascination with the famous Burr-Hamilton duel. One of the earliest American photographs, owned by the Pennsylvania Historical Society, is of this grave. It was taken in 1854, and the photographer himself is seated on the nearby grave of Samuel Davies, fourth president of the college.

President Grover Cleveland must have been an unusually modest politician. The inscription on his grave stone simply says:

Grover Cleveland
Born Caldwell, N.J.
March 18th 1837
Died Princeton, N.J.
June 24th 1908

Frequently, someone campaigns to place a marker in recognition of the two terms he served in the White House. As his son has often stated, it was his father's wish that no mention be made of that fact on his grave. Princeton Cemetery has been steadfast in honoring that request.

The smaller monument marks the grave of Ruth Cleveland who died in 1904 at age thirteen. Her name is perhaps better known than

Publisher: Christie Whiteman, Princeton, NJ, Card No. 6586 12 E 46 * Manufacturer: Made in Germany * Type: Colored, Divided Back * Postmark: Not Used * Value Index: C

her father's, because she was always called "Baby Ruth." Yes, that's right, the candy bar was named for her.

Witherspoon Presbyterian Church, in the background, was founded to serve the Black neighborhood. When Paul Robeson was born, his father, William Drew Robeson, was pastor of this church. Both parents are buried within a short distance of the spot shown in this picture.

Except for the dirt street and the horse and buggy, this picture of Vandeventer Avenue could almost be duplicated today. The imposing Wiggins Street House facing this street at the far end looks the same.

The house in the right foreground has been radically remodeled with the front porch removed and the entire roof line altered. The only recognizable portion extant is the two-story bay wing section behind the small tree.

Not too many years before, this entire area was part of the J. Van Deventer Nurseries. At the left, towards Wiggins Street, were two sizeable ponds. Undoubtedly, the water was rechanneled into the underground stream which meanders east through the town. As you will note, the spelling of

Publisher: The Temme Co., Orange, NJ (F.G.T. Co. Series) Card No. 2 C 52 * Manufacturer: Made in Germany * Type: Colored, Divided Back * Postmark: September 16, 1911 * Value Index: E

the name has been modified, but the street name is pronounced in an unusual way. The accent is on the second syllable; why?

People driving in and out of Princeton today would be ecstatic if this peaceful scene could return. They would probably accept this smooth dirt road for the existing potholes.

At some point in the history of Princeton, Washington Street became Washington Road. It is still the principal road of the three roads that enter Princeton from the south. Coming from the New Jersey Turnpike and U.S. Route 1, it funnels tractor trailers and other vehicles through the Princeton University campus, down Nassau Street through the heart of town, to connect with New Jersey Route 206 at the west end of town. As a result, Princeton is no longer a quiet college town.

WASHINGTON ST. SHOWING CARNEGIE LAKE, PRINCETON, N. J.

Publisher: Christie Whiteman, Princeton, NJ * Manufacturer: Not Indicated * Type: Colored, White Border, Divided Back * Postmark: Not Used * Value Index: E

Until 1966, Princeton Borough and Princeton Township had separate school systems, although the Township sent their high school students to the Borough's high school. In the first decade of the 20th century, the Model School shown on this Postcard, plus two smaller "annexes" nearby, housed Kindergarten through 12th Grades for the Borough, except for the black elementary students who attended the Witherspoon School on Quarry Street (now a nursing home). In 1910, the total enrollment was 563 students, which included 88 in the high school. Clearly, about 60 percent of the students did not complete high school, which was normal in that era. Unless a youngster planned to attend college, an eighth grade education was considered sufficient to enter the work force. Today, virtually

"MODEL" PUBLIC SCHOOL, PRINCETON, N. J.

Pub. by Edw. G. van Marter

Publisher: Edw. G. van Marter, Princeton, NJ * Manufacturer: Printed in Germany * Type: Colored, Divided Back * Postmark: Not Used * Value Index: D

all the Princeton High School students earn diplomas, and the vast majority continue into college or other advanced training.

There are no old postcards of the Witherspoon School or the Township schools in the author's collection. It is possible that none were ever printed because of the limited market.

Although this postcard is identified as the "Princeton Model School," this school was built next door, to the east of the original Model School. "The Princeton Directory 1910-1911" explains that, "The school having completely outgrown its present accommodations, the citizens of the borough have recently voted the sum of $65,000 for the erection of a new building with modern school equipment and a Gymnasium. It is hoped that the building will be ready for occupancy by September 1911." At a later date, an addition was built at the right; the old school was razed to provide room for the addition. With the construction of the present high school in 1929, this building

PRINCETON MODEL SCHOOL, PRINCETON, N. J.

Publisher: E.J. Van Marter, Princeton, NJ * Manufacturer: Photochrome G & S * Type: Colored, Divided Back * Postmark: Not Used * Value Index: D

was renamed "Nassau Street School." All of the white Borough students through the 8th Grade attended this school until the late 1940s when the new New Jersey State Constitution required that the schools be integrated. Until 1966, Nassau Street School was Kindergarten through 5th Grade, and the formerly segregated Witherspoon School contained the 6th through 8th Grades for all Borough students. When the John Witherspoon School on Walnut Lane opened in 1966, this building was sold to Princeton University and is now identified as 185 Nassau Street.

Today, this continuation of Nassau Street is known as Princeton-Kingston Road. When the picture was taken, the newly constructed Carnegie Lake (indicated in the postcard as Princeton Lake) crept toward the road at the right. From the left, Harry's Brook drains under the road into the lake. The small stone bridge which carries the roadway over the brook is currently the center of controversy. The State of New Jersey wishes to replace it with a modern concrete structure, but many Princetonians want to preserve the charm of the unobtrusive stone bridge. Local citizens have underwritten an engineering survey which purports to show that the little bridge can be strengthened and repaired for considerably less than the cost of a replacement. The

Copyrighted 1907, by W. C. Sinclair   KINGSTON ROAD, PRINCETON LAKE

Publisher: W. C. Sinclair, Princeton, NJ * Manufacturer: Not Indicated * Type: Black and White, Undivided Back * Postmark: 1909 * Value Index: C

last shot has not yet been fired in this battle. This postcard clearly shows the rural nature of Princeton Township in 1907. Despite the fact that the road is part of a principal artery between Trenton and New Brunswick, it is not much better than the rutted highway of the 1700s. There are signs of habitation in the distance, near the Kingston Mill, but the land to the left has now been converted into a suburban area by the post-World War II housing boom. The land to the right belongs to Princeton University; the crew races end just beyond the spit of land.

In 1905, Woodrow Wilson, President of Princeton University, introduced a method of instruction whereby small groups of students were led and guided in their studies by a new group of faculty members called Preceptors. The requirements of this plan immediately doubled the size of the faculty. Moses Taylor Pyne, a trustee, realized the housing difficulties faced by the Preceptors and purchased land in the Broadmead section in the northeast section of Princeton. There he built 23 homes which he leased for nominal rents.

This photograph shows the entrance to Broadmead from Princeton Avenue. Local residents dubbed the development "White City," because the stucco on all of the Tudor-style homes

Entrance, White City, Broadmead, Princeton, N. J.

Publisher: Van Marter, Princeton, NJ * Manufacturer: Printed in Germany * Type: Colored, Divided Back * Postmark: Not Used * Value Index: C

was painted white. It is obvious that Princeton Avenue in the foreground is a brand new street. The contractor has not yet had an opportunity to install the finished paving. Except for growth of the trees and the fact that the houses are not mud-colored, the view is the same today.

The lack of trees and limited shrubbery show that the Broadmead houses were still new when this picture was taken. Moses Taylor Pyne was a devotee of the Tudor style of architecture. Other examples are the Upper and Lower Pyne buildings which are shown elsewhere in this book. At his death, the entire development was bequeathed to Princeton University.

By late 1900 standards, these three-story houses would be considered spacious, to say the least. It is said that when they were built, they were considered modest homes, because they required only three servants to care for them.

The White City, Broadmead, Princeton, N. J.

Publisher: Van Marter, Princeton, NJ * Manufacturer: Printed in Germany * Type: Colored, Divided Back * Postmark: Not Used * Value Index: C

After the Quaker Meeting House was built in 1724, and the Presbyterian Church was organized in 1766, almost 70 years elapsed before another denomination of the Christian Church established a congregation in Princeton. Under the leadership of Captain Robert ("Fighting Bob") Stockton, grandson of Richard "The Signer", Trinity Episcopal Church was organized. The church opened its doors in 1834.

The original church building was in the popular Greek Revival style. With its massive pillars, it resembled the Presbyterian Church and the Theological Seminary's Miller Chapel. The resemblance was probably not coincidental, because all three structures were built by Charles Steadman, a prolific local builder. Many of the buildings designed and built by Steadman have been preserved. They command a premium on the local real estate market.

The Steadman church building was razed in 1868 to be replaced by the Gothic building shown in this photograph. In turn, this building underwent major alterations and additions in 1914-1915. Its overall appearance was vastly improved by redesigning the rather squat steeple along more graceful lines.

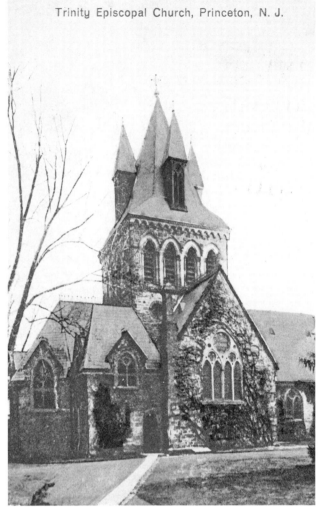

Trinity Episcopal Church, Princeton, N. J.

Publisher: Van Marter, Princeton, NJ, Card No. 2489/30 * Manufacturer: Printed in Germany * Type: Colored, Divided Back * Postmark: April 20, 1914 * Value Index: D

Publisher: Not Indicated * Manufacturer: Not Indicated * Type: Real Photograph, Divided Back * Postmark: Not Used * Value Index: B

On the old postcards, interior views are relatively uncommon. This photograph shows the chancel of Trinity Episcopal Church, although it is difficult to determine whether the picture was taken before or after the 1914-1915 renovations.

In the spring of 1963, a fire gutted most of the church sanctuary, including the organ loft. At approximately the same time, there was a liturgical renewal in the denomination which resulted in moving the altar forward in front of the lecterns. The reason for the change was to bring the altar among the people, rather than be separated by the choir stalls in the chancel. The choir loft is now in the rear of the sanctuary.

Originally, settlement of the Princeton area began at the two extreme ends of town. Henry Greenland, surgeon and innkeeper, settled at the eastern end near Kingston. To the west, a group of Quaker families cleared farms along the Stony Brook. According to one author, the name "Princeton" was first applied to the area in 1724, which was the same year that the Chesterfield Monthly Meeting of Friends authorized the construction of a meeting house. After a serious fire during the 1750s, the existing building was constructed on the original foundation. The Quaker Meeting House is the oldest religious structure in Princeton. In the early days, it was the center of the religious, social and political life of the community. In the grave-

Publisher: W. C. Sinclair, Princeton, NJ * Manufacturer: The Albertype Co., Brooklyn, NY * Type: Black and White, Divided Back * Postmark: Not Used * Value Index: E

yard behind the stone wall are the remains of Richard Stockton, Signer of the Declaration of Independence. In conformance with the Quaker religious tradition of the time, the grave is unmarked. The meeting house was used as a hospital after the Battle of Princeton. As the town center shifted into the orbit of the College of New Jersey, and as other churches became established, the numbers of Quakers declined. By the 1870s, the meeting house was closed, but it was reopened after World War II. It is home for an active religious community.

Early in the 19th century, the Presbyterian Church next to the college was struggling for existence. It was caught up in an acrimonious denominational schism during the 1830s. In addition, it was having financial problems, and the congregation was unhappy with its pastor. From this turmoil, twelve men "separated" from First Presbyterian Church in 1847 to found the Second Presbyterian Church, later renamed St. Andrews.

The new congregation built a frame church at 190-192 Nassau Street. When the congregation moved to its new building on the corner of Chambers and Nassau Streets in 1868, the original was rotated on its lot so that it was parallel to Nassau Street, and was converted to a double house. At least a portion of the structure remains

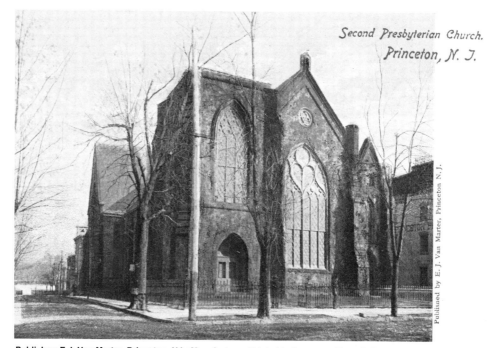

Publisher: E.J. Van Marter, Princeton, NJ * Manufacturer: Printed in Germany * Type: Colored, Undivided Back * Postmark: Not Used * Value Index: E

today as the rear wing of an office building at that spot. The plans for the new church called for a tall slender spire on the corner over the main entrance, but the design was never carried to completion.

Several attempts were made to reunite the two churches, without success. The 1905 failure prompted Woodrow Wilson to transfer his membership over to First Presbyterian Church. Reunion was finally accomplished in 1973 under the new name of Nassau Presbyterian Church. The former St. Andrews building is now the home of the Nassau Christian Center.

Publisher: Van Marter, Princeton, NJ * Manufacturer: Not Indicated * Type: Black and White, Colored Imprint, Undivided Back * Postmark: Not Used * Value Index: D

Publisher: Christie Whiteman, Princeton, NJ, Card No. B 9916 * Manufacturer: American News Co., NY, Leipzig, Dresden, Berlin, "Excelsior" (Made in Germany) * Type: Black and White, Divided Back * Postmark: Not Used * Value Index: C

The present Nassau Presbyterian Church (formerly First Presbyterian) is the third building on this site. After the College of New Jersey moved to Princeton in 1756, local Presbyterians worshipped with the college community in the Prayer Room of Nassau Hall. As the town grew, residents wanted a church of their own, and the college needed a larger auditorium for commencements. Negotiations stemming from these needs led to agreement that a sanctuary would be built on college land. Ultimately, the land was deeded to the church, and it was agreed that one side of the galleries would be reserved for students, the college could use the building at specified times, and the church land would not be used as a burial ground. That burial ground is now the "old section" of the Princeton Cemetery.

The first two church buildings were plagued with misfortune. During the Revolution, the building was stripped and almost destroyed by occupying troops of both the British and Colonial Armies. With the economy in disarray, it was not fully restored for many years. Finally, in 1813, a sexton was careless with live coals, and the church burned to the ground. The second building was also the victim of carelessness. In 1835, during an Independence Day celebration, a wayward rocket landed on the roof, and the church was again destroyed by fire.

The photograph shows the third building, designed and built by Charles Steadman, the famous local builder. When the building was extended to the rear in 1907, Princeton University donated land and money with the proviso that the wing shown at the right be torn down because it "had obscured the view from Nassau Street to some of the buildings." The wrought iron fence in the foreground went to the metal scrap drive in World War II, and the gas-lit street light at the curb is long gone. Fortunately, the present-day church has been spared the intrusion of parking meters.

The origin of the Princeton Methodist Episcopal Church was a small church in Cedar Grove, a tiny settlement in Princeton Township. The principal financial support of that church was provided by Paul Tulane, a philanthropic native of the area. His contributions were legendary, and included an endowment of a small college in Louisiana that led to today's Tulane University. He supported many local causes, including the First Presbyterian Church. On at least one occasion, however, the Presbyterians may have gone to the well once too often. Mr. Tulane paid the requested contribution, but he made the check out to "That Damned Old Presbyterian Church - Again." For many years, Princeton Bank had the framed check hanging in its offices.

Although there were few Methodists in the town of Princeton, the decision was made to build the new church on Nassau Street. Apparently some residents were opposed, because the trustees had to use subterfuge to acquire the land. Dr. Oliver Bartine lived on the northeast corner of Nassau Street and Vandeventer Avenue. On the pretext of enlarging the grounds around his office, he purchased the adjoining property; it was promptly conveyed to the new church. Ironically, a few years later, Dr. Bartine was deprived of his church membership for failure to attend class meetings! Obviously, the 19th century Methodists tolerated no nonsense.

The original building served well for over 50 years, but the growth of the congregation led to a decision to replace it. Funding proved to be difficult, but two major contributions cleared the way. Charles H. Sanford, a friend of the pastor pledged a large sum, and Moses Taylor Pyne donated the corner property next to the church. Only nineteen months elapsed between the last service in the original structure and the dedication of the new church in 1911. During that time, a temporary "Plank Chapel" was built, the house on the corner lot was moved to 25 Vandeventer Avenue, and the granite church shown in this photograph was erected—all with minimal interruption to the church activities.

In terms of building activity, St. Paul Roman Catholic Church has had an eventful history. When it was instituted in 1850, land was purchased at 182 Nassau Street (where Cox's store now stands). To begin construction, the priest and men of the parish dug the cellar of the new church, presumably by hand, completing it in one day. The church was completed in a short time and after the new church was in use for a few years, the floor under the altar collapsed during a service. The building was declared unsafe, abandoned, and razed.

The current property was purchased in 1859. A new church and school were created by additions and alterations to an existing house. Then, in 1869-1870, the church shown on this postcard was constructed. Major remodeling in 1912 extended the front of the church, enlarged the entrances, and added a new bell tower. Finally, in 1955 it was discovered that the foundations had become weakened and the support beams were beyond repair. The building was torn down, and the present stone church was dedicated in 1957.

The fate of the 1859 church and rectory buildings is interesting. They were sold in 1890 and were moved across Nassau Street to Charlton Street. The front section is now No. 6 and No. 8 Charlton Street and the rear section is No. 10 and No. 12 Charlton Street.

Publisher: Van Marter, Princeton, NJ * Manufacturer: Not Indicated * Type: Black and White, Colored Imprint, Undivided Back * Postmark: Not Used * Value Index: D

THE RECTORY, ST. PAUL'S CATHOLIC CHURCH, PRINCETON, N. J.   Pub. by Van Marter

The house shown in the photograph was the third rectory for St. Paul Church. It was built in 1874 and stood facing Nassau Street approximately in front of the present rectory. The church stood behind the trees at the right. The parochial school was farther east on the same spot as the present school building. This photograph dates from approximately 1905. In the ensuing years, the rectory was enlarged and remodeled. Finally, in the 1950s the parish concluded that the church rectory and convent needed costly major repairs and the buildings were inadequate to accommodate the steady parish growth. In a complicated series of moves, the Sisters moved from the

Publisher: Van Marter, Princeton, NJ * Manufacturer: Not Indicated * Type: Black and White, Divided Back * Postmark: Not Used * Value Index: A

convent to the rectory, the old convent was razed, the church was demolished, a new convent was erected on the foundation of the church, and the present rectory was built. Upon completion of the new convent in 1956, the 1874 rectory was demolished. The entire St. Paul complex was completed in 1957 with the dedication of the new church building.

When you travel west from Princeton on Stockton Street, you will note this little stone wellhead standing by the street. The stone cap, now cracked and broken, is carved with the legend, "Washington Spring, A.D. 1776." According to tradition, General Washington paused to refresh himself at the spring following the Battle of Princeton.

The trim pathway was useful in a pedestrian age, but it no longer exists. The marble pillars at the end of the hedge framed the narrow driveway entering Drumthwacket, the home of Moses Taylor Pyne, who is so often mentioned throughout this text.

The Washington Spring, A. D. 1776.   Princeton, N. J.

Publisher: H. M. Hinkson, Stationer, Princeton, NJ * Manufacturer: The Albertype Co., Brooklyn, NY * Type: Black and White, Divided Back * Postmark: Not Used * Value Index: D

Pyne Gateway, Princeton, N. J.

Publisher: Christie Whiteman, Princeton, NJ, Card No. E4343 * Manufacturer: American News Co., NY, Leipzig, Berlin, Dresden, "Quarto-Chrome," Made in Germany * Type: Colored, Divided Back * Postmark: Not Used * Value Index: C

This striking marble gateway was an entrance to Drumthwacket, the estate of Moses Taylor Pyne, wealthy alumnus and trustee of Princeton University. The gravel drive meandered through a dense grove of trees before it approached the Pyne residence. It also served the numerous outbuildings and finally exited onto Mercer Street.

The vestigial remnants of the gateway remain standing on Stockton Street, several hundred feet to the west of the present entrance. The wrought iron gates and smaller side pillars are gone; the main pillars have been sawed off to less than one-half of their original height. As a result, all that is visible today is a pair of stumpy worn marble markers.

The pillared center section of this mansion was built in 1833 by Charles Olden, descendant of one of the original Princeton Quaker families, and Governor of New Jersey (1860-1863). Moses Taylor Pyne acquired the property in the 1890s. He added the two wings to the original residence, and he also enlarged the grounds to a total of 300 acres. From Lovers Lane on the east to Stony Brook on the west, all of the land between Stockton Street and Mercer Street was included in the estate, which he named Drumthwacket ("Wooded Hill").

RESIDENCE M. TAYLOR PYNE, PRINCETON, N. J.   Pub. by Van Marter

Publisher: Van Marter, Princeton, NJ * Manufacturer: Not Indicated * Type: Black and White, Undivided Back * Postmark: Not Used * Value Index: C

According to his contemporaries, Pyne developed the estate into a feudal manor. It was a working farm, complete with stables, barns, greenhouses, and homes for his staff. It is better remembered, however, for its spacious mansion, the aviary in the old 18th century house near Stockton Street, the deer park, the formal Italian gardens, and the beautifully landscaped park with its numerous paths. Pyne was known as a benevolent "Lord of the Manor," and Drumthwacket was a center for the social life of both the town and the University. Visitors were welcome to stroll through the gardens and grounds.

In 1941, after the death of Pyne's widow, the estate was sold. In 1966, the mansion and twelve acres of land were purchased by the State of New Jersey. The property has been restored for use as the official governor's residence with Governor Florio the first New Jersey chief executive to live there.

Immediately in back of Drumthwacket, the slope of the land to the south was elaborately terraced. The first terrace, behind the stone balustrade shown in the photograph, was a wide lawn shaded by five great sycamores. A short flight of steps led down to the Italian garden with its ornate fountain. Reputedly, all of the gardens were cared for by squads of skilled Italian gardeners. To the right of the picture, (not shown) is the next level which contained a tennis court and a lawn bowling green. One effusive author said that there were "green topiary chairs, looking comfortable enough to sit in, and peacocks which stir in the breeze as if preparing to dodge a chance tennis ball." Note the watchful St. Bernard dog sitting on the path.

M. T. Pynes Italian Garden, Princeton, N. J.

Publisher: W. C. Sinclair, Princeton, NJ, Card No. A 4717 * Manufacturer: American News Co., NY, Leipzig, Dresden, Berlin, "Excelsior," Made in Germany * Type: Black and White, Divided Back * Postmark: Not Used * Value Index: E

This white marble fountain, which one writer termed a "treasure trove from Italy", was the focal point of the formal gardens at Drumthwacket. Originally commissioned by a noble family of Padua as a gift to the Republic of Venice, it never left Padua until it was purchased by Pyne for his manor. In Pyne's era, wealthy men scoured the old world for treasures to incorporate into their estates. Probably the most notable example was William Randolph Hearst's San Simeon.

Fountain in M. T. Pynes Italian Garden, Princeton, N. J.

Publisher: W. C. Sinclair, Princeton, NJ, Card No. A 4713 * Manufacturer: American News Co., NY, Leipzig, Dresden, Berlin, "Excelsior," Made in Germany * Type: Black and White, Divided Back * Postmark: Not Used * Value Index: E

An integral element of Mr. Pyne's landscaping was the damming of a small brook to form four ponds. This photograph clearly illustrates the attention to detail which characterized the entire manor. The beautiful little stone bridge carried the path across the water at the foot of the small stone dam. Imagine the pleasure experienced by visitors on hot summer days when their stroll took them within a few feet of the waterfall.

The first of the ponds was accented with a small Greek Temple. The other ponds were unadorned except for the dams and foot bridges. Pyne completed the beauty of the scene by providing a pair of swans for each pond.

M. T. Pynes Estate. Princeton, N. J.

Publisher: W. C. Sinclair, Princeton, NJ * Manufacturer: The Albertype Co., Brooklyn, NY * Type: Black and White, Divided Back * Postmark: Not Used * Value Index: D

The thickly wooded area behind Drumthwacket was separated from the formal gardens by the first of the four ponds. The gardens were carefully replanted according to the season of the year. The woods were landscaped to provide continuously changing colors of shrubs and wild flowers. The paths wound among the trees and along the water for enjoyment by all guests and visitors. This photograph illustrates the placid flow of the stream with the pathway adjacent to it. Note the carefully tended path and the trim bank by the dam.

Publisher: W. C. Sinclair, Princeton, NJ * Manufacturer: The Albertype Co., Brooklyn, NY * Type: Black and White, Divided Back * Postmark: Not Used * Value Index: D

The pond shown in the photograph is undoubtedly the last and smallest of the four ponds on the Drumthwacket property. In the distance is Moses Taylor Pyne's home, and to the left is one of the ubiquitous pathways. From the size of this particular pond, it seems safe to assume that it was the one once used for tryouts by the Princeton University ice hockey team. Of course, that was long before the advent of Baker Rink.

In the right background, with fencing in the lower terrace, there was a tall hemlock hedge. An arched opening in the hedge provided visitors with an unobstructed view of the fields, the ponds, and the farm.

Publisher: H. M. Hinkson, Stationer, Princeton, NJ * Manufacturer: The Albertype Co., Brooklyn, NY * Type: Black and White, Divided Back * Postmark: Not Used * Value Index: D

It is difficult to determine the specific point from which this panoramic picture of the Drumthwacket grounds was taken. The photograph plainly illustrates the pastoral beauty of Pyne's manor. The well-maintained driveway and park-like grounds attest to the meticulous care exercised by his gardeners, farmers, and other staff.

The sheep had a dual function on this farm/estate. They were a source of meat and they also served as living lawn mowers in the fields. Pyne also had a herd of deer which served the same purpose.

View in M. T. Pynes Grounds, Princeton, N. J.

Publisher: W. C. Sinclair, Princeton, NJ, Card No. 7835 * Manufacturer: American News Co., NY, Leipzig, Dresden, Berlin, "Excelsior," Made in Germany * Type: Black and White, Divided Back * Postmark: Not Used * Value Index: D

The correct name for this mansion is Constitution Hill. It was built by Junius Morgan, cousin of J. P. Morgan, Sr., in 1896. Although he razed the original pre-Revolutionary house which stood on this spot, he retained the old name for the property. Tradition claims that the New Jersey Constitution was drafted there in 1776. Princeton could boast of numerous elaborate "Manor Houses." Unfortunately, comparatively few were pictured on early Postcards.

Constitution Hill was owned and occupied by the Morgan Family until the 1970s, when it was sold to the same firm which redeveloped the Palmer Square area.

CONSTITUTION HALL, PRINCETON, N. J.   Pub. by Van Marter

Publisher: Van Marter, Princeton, NJ * Manufacturer: Not Indicated * Type: Black and White, Undivided Back * Postmark: Not Used * Value Index: E

The property is now a luxury condominium complex with a total of 52 living units. Of these, eight are in the 1896 buildings—four in the main house, two in the squash court, and two in the stables and garage.

Often described as "New Jersey's Most Historic House," Morven was owned by the Stocktons for almost two centuries. The house was built by Richard Stockton ("Richard the Signer") in 1754. During the revolution, Stockton was taken prisoner and was later exchanged by the British after a personal appeal by General Washington. When the Continental Congress fled to Princeton in the summer of 1783, Annis Stockton, Richard's widow, hosted a scintillating July 4th dinner party. All of the members of Congress were included, and General and Mrs. Washington were among the guests. Quite a party for a town of only a few hundred residents!

In 1945, Walter E. Edge, Governor of New Jersey, pur-

"Morven", The Home of Richard Stockton, the Signer of the Declaration of Independence   Princeton, N. J.

Publisher: H. M. Hinkson, Stationer, Princeton, NJ * Manufacturer: The Albertype Co., Brooklyn, NY * Type: Black and White, Divided Back * Postmark: Not Used * Value Index: E

chased Morven. He recognized the historic significance of his home and deeded it to the State of New Jersey in 1951 for use as a Governor's Residence or museum. Ultimately, it became obvious that it was inadequate for the Governor's needs. Drumthwacket was then designated as the official residence, and Morven became a museum. Subsequently, it underwent an extensive archaeological dig. One objective of the dig was to determine how the grounds and out-buildings were designed by Richard and Annis Stockton in the 1700s.

In 1768, at the call of the College of New Jersey, John Witherspoon emigrated from Scotland to the village of Princeton to assume the presidency of the young college. He quickly became an outspoken patriot and served in the Continental Congress from 1776 to 1782. Thus, he joined Richard Stockton in becoming the second Princeton signer of the Declaration of Independence. After the Revolution, he struggled to restore both the buildings and the enrollment of the college. Also, he was a delegate to the state convention which ratified the Federal Constitution, and he was active in the formation of the new national organization of the Presbyterian Church. It is

"Tusculum", Home of John Witherspoon. Princeton, N. J.   Home of Dr. M. W. Pardee ...   Built 1773

Publisher: W. C. Sinclair, Princeton, NJ * Manufacturer: The Albertype Co., Brooklyn, NY * Type: Black and White, Divided Back * Postmark: Not Used * Value Index: C

understandable that he ranks as a giant among the presidents of the College of New Jersey and Princeton University.

A life-long interest in farming led him to build Tusculum a short distance from town. Today's Witherspoon Street was the first portion of the route to his farm on Cherry Hill Road. In this photograph, the simple stone farmhouse of colonial times is scarcely discernible behind the later Victorian "improvements" to the facade.

Note how the words "Home of Dr. M. W. Pardee, formerly . . ." and "Built 1773" have been carelessly over-printed with the original caption. Dr. Pardee was a well-known local dentist at the beginning of the 20th century.

The motif of Victorian clutter obviously extended to the grounds of Tusculum. Fortunately, the curlicues and gingerbread loved by the Victorians have been removed. In the 1930s, the house was carefully remodeled to restore its original colonial simplicity.

The Tusculum property has been in the local headlines with another battle between land developers and preservation forces; the latter appear to have won. The land may be saved for public open space, and the house will probably continue under private ownership.

Publisher: Edw. J. Van Marter, Princeton, NJ, Card No. 2027/2, 8731 * Manufacturer: N. N., Distributed by E. W. Fausnaugh, Printed in Germany * Type: Colored, Divided Back * Postmark: Not Used * Value Index: C

Near the end of his second term, United States President Grover Cleveland was a key speaker at the 150th anniversary celebration when the College of New Jersey was officially renamed Princeton University. He became a friend of Andrew Fleming West, who had invited him to speak. Both President and Mrs. Cleveland fell in love with the small college town, and they decided to retire in Princeton. West helped the President to acquire the house shown in this photograph, and President Cleveland named it Westland for his friend.

Several years after the end of World War II, the house was still owned by the Cleveland estate. When it was sold, a section behind the portion of the

Grover Cleveland's Res., Princeton, N. J.

Publisher: Illustrated Postal Card Co., New York—Germany, Card No. 99-12 * Manufacturer: Illustrated Postal Card Co., New York—Germany * Type: Colored, Undivided Back * Postmark: Not Used * Value Index: E

house shown in the photograph was razed. As a result, two homes were created suitable for 20th century living.

Today, the house looks almost the same as in the photograph, with one unfortunate exception. The small porch and pillars at the right have been removed, and the shuttered windows have been replaced by blank double doors opening into a garage that was created in that wing.

Four homes occupied by Woodrow Wilson and his family remain today in Princeton. When he joined the faculty of his alma mater in 1889, he rented the house at 72 Library Place. Within a few years, he designed and built a house nearby at 82 Library Place. Of course, while he was President of Princeton University, the family lived on the campus at Prospect, the official presidential residence.

When he resigned from the university to become Governor of New Jersey, he moved to 25 Cleveland Lane, which is the house shown in the photograph. After he moved to the White House in 1912, the family never lived in Princeton again, although President Wilson retained his voting residence at the Nassau Street home of Professor Stockton Axson, his brother-in-Law.

PRINCETON HOME OF "PRESIDENT WILSON", PRINCETON, N. J.

Publisher: Christie Whiteman, Princeton, NJ * Manufacturer: Probably Curt Teich Co., Chicago, IL * Type: Colored, White Border, Divided Back * Postmark: Not Used * Value Index: E

In the first third of the 20th century, Henry van Dyke—theologian, professor, poet, lecturer, essayist, story teller, and diplomat—was a world-renowned member of the Princeton University faculty. When he returned to Princeton in 1899, he lived in this beautiful mansion, Avalon, on Bayard Lane. There is speculation that a portion of the house had been built in the 18th century when it was owned by an uncle of Commodore Bainbridge of "Constitution" ("Old Ironsides") fame. In the 1950s, the building was razed to make room for the new YMCA/YWCA.

As might be expected in a history-conscious town, the destruction of a historic house was not popular. A committee of townspeople studied the alternatives. The conclusion of their efforts was that cumulative neglect made the cost of restoration prohibitive. Fortunately, the library was salvaged and was moved to Connecticut by the van Dyke Family.

Dr. Henry Van Dyke's Residence, Princeton, N.J.

Publisher: Van Marter, Princeton, NJ, Card No. 868/6 * Manufacturer: N. N., Distributed by E. W. Fausnaugh, Printed in Germany * Type: Colored, Divided Back * Postmark: July 21, 1910 * Value Index: E

When the YMCA/YWCA was built, the town created a new section of street from Bayard Lane to John Street and named it Avalon Place. However, even that reminder of the past has disappeared. It has been renamed Paul Robeson Place after the famous singer/actor who was born in Princeton.

Colonel William Libbey, Jr., built his massive stone residence, Thanet Lodge, next door to Dr. van Dyke's Avalon on a former college playing field. Although he was a distinguished professor, he is probably better remembered for other facets of his life. He was the first to receive a doctoral degree from the College of New Jersey, and he collaborated with Moses Taylor Pyne to compile the first alumni directory for the college. A most interesting incident, however, was the role he played in the adoption of orange and black as the Princeton school colors. Although orange had been a college color since 1868, the combined orange and black began when freshman William Libbey, Jr., purchased a thousand yards of orange and black silk ribbon for distribution at a regatta

Col. Libby's Residence, Princeton. N. J.

Publisher: Van Marter, Princeton, NJ, Card No 868/1 * Manufacturer: N.N., Distributed by E.W. Faunsnaugh, Printed in Germany * Type: Colored, Divided Back * Postmark: Not Used * Value Index: D

held in Saratoga, New York. The students quickly adopted the colors for their athletic teams, songs, and other activities. When the college became Princeton University in 1896, the trustees formally adopted the colors, even though some of the faculty objected.

It is not surprising that Princeton Theological Seminary's Alexander Hall resembles Nassau Hall at Princeton University. The seminary's roots were in the Presbyterian dominated College of New Jersey, and it was founded in 1811 with the aid and encouragement of the college. The college felt that its growth was being inhibited by the Presbyterians, and the Presbyterians were disturbed by the secular trends in the college life and curriculum. As one of the early professors wrote, they wanted to have a "divinity school uncontaminated by the college."

Unlike the vicissitudes endured by Nassau Hall, Alexander Hall has not suffered from students' bombs and riots.

Alexander Hall. Princeton Theological Seminary.

Publisher: W. C. Sinclair, Princeton, NJ * Manufacturer: The Albertype Co., Brooklyn, NY * Type: Black and White, Divided Back * Postmark: Not Used * Value Index: E

The most serious threat to the building was a New Year's Day fire in 1913. A student had stayed over for the holidays and was cooking in his room at the center of the fourth floor. The resulting fire destroyed the cupola; the replacement is much more imposing than the original.

One casualty of the fire was the bell in the cupola, which had signalled students to class for 85 years. To raise money for the repairs, an enterprising individual collected the bell fragments and had small handbells cast from the metal. The bells were then sold to the alumni.

This postcard of Miller Chapel shows it in its original location facing Mercer Street. At the right is the eastern end of Alexander Hall, and the tower of Stuart Hall can be seen in the left background. The hedge leading to the steps of the chapel screened the Archibald Alexander house, which is the home built in 1821 for the first seminary professor. The chapel dates from 1833, and 100 years later, in 1933, it was moved back on the campus and turned 90 degrees to face the green behind Alexander Hall. At the same time, it was enlarged and restored, as far as possible, to its original design. In 1874, it had been "improved" with heavy Victorian touches such as stained glass windows and upholstered pews. Because the seminary did not have any pictures of the

Publisher: Christie Whiteman, Princeton, NJ * Manufacturer: Not Indicated * Type: Sepia, Divided Back * Postmark: April 18, 1911 * Value Index: C

original interior, the 1933 remodeled sanctuary was almost completely new in design. An interesting touch is the glass used in the windows. To conform to the age of the building, hand rolled glass was installed, and it has the faintly lavender tint associated with old glass.

Hodge Hall, built in 1893, was featured in the local news. For 87 years, residents of Room 400 in this dormitory recorded their names and years on the inside wall of a closet. Miraculously, in the maintenance of the room over that long period, painters respected the scrawled request, "Don't ever paint in this space." The list was obliterated in 1980 during a major renovation, but the tradition was immediately restored with the new plea, "Please never paint here."

The unusual v-shaped configuration of the dormitory stems from a stipulation addended to the gift which began its construction. The donor specified that every room should have the benefit of sunlight at some time during the day.

Charles Hodge, for whom the building is named, was a giant among 19th century theologians for more than 50 years. He was an eloquent spokesman for, and defender of, rigid conservatism of the seminary in that era. He once summed up his theological position with the rather startling statement, "I am not afraid to say that a new idea never originated in this seminary."

Publisher: W. C. Sinclair, Princeton, NJ, Card No. B3144 * Manufacturer: American News Co., NY, Leipzig, Dresden, Berlin, "Excelsior," Made in Germany * Type: Black and White, Divided Back * Postmark: April 7, 1909 * Value Index: D

Brown Hall (1864) was the first dormitory built by the Princeton Theological Seminary, and it continues today to house "Seminoles" (as the college students used to call the seminarians). At a cost of $30,000, construction took place during the difficult Civil War years. A contemporary author described it as "A large and handsome stone dormitory."

The building was a gift from Mrs. Isabella Brown of Baltimore, Maryland. She was the first female to donate a building to either the college or the seminary.

Brown Hall.   Princeton Theological Seminary.

Publisher: H. M. Hinkson, Stationer, Princeton, NJ * Manufacturer: The Albertype Co., Brooklyn, NY * Type: Black and White, Divided Back * Postmark: July 2, 1924 * Value Index: E

The caption on this postcard should say "Stuart Hall" rather than "Stewart Hall." This general lecture and classroom building was given to the seminary by two brothers, Messrs. Robert L. and Alexander Stuart, in 1876, at a cost of $140,000. At the time of its completion, historian John Frelinghaysen Hageman wrote, "This is the best constructed building in Princeton, as to workmanship, and perhaps also as to style and adaptation."

In the 1940s, the tower was judged to be unsafe, and it was removed.

In the 1980s, the entire building was refurbished, remodeled, and restored.

It is obvious that the Stuart brothers were devout Presbyterians in the mold of Charles Hodge. A limitation in the

Publisher: Not Indicated * Manufacturer: Not Indicated * Type: Photograph, Divided Back * Postmark: Not Used * Value Index: C

deed to Stuart Hall specifies if four doctrines declared by the Confession of Faith and Catechism of the Presbyterian Church "shall cease to be taught and inculcated," the property shall revert to the Stuart heirs. Six specific doctrines were listed.

The untitled photograph shows the original Lenox Library on the Princeton Theological Seminary Campus. The donor, James Lenox was a wealthy bibliophile who served as trustee of both the seminary and the college. Erected in 1843, it was the third seminary building (following Alexander Hall and Miller Chapel), and it was the first library building built by any institution in Princeton. When he wrote his famous Princeton history in the 1870s, John Frelinghaysen Hageman described it as an "exquisitely beautiful Gothic structure," and commented, "The whole is one of the most correct and beautiful specimens of Gothic architecture in our country."

Publisher: Not Indicated * Manufacturer: Not Indicated * Type: Photograph, Divided Back * Postmark: Not Used * Value Index: B

Because Mr. Lenox also gave the second library, there has been some confusion over the names of the two buildings. The Gothic building facing Mercer Street was originally called Lenox Hall, but was familiarly known as Lenox Library. When the new library was built, it assumed the Lenox Library name, and the older building was simply called the Reference Library.

Both of the 19th century libraries were destroyed in the 1950s and replaced by Speer Library.

James Lenox also underwrote the construction of the second seminary library, completed in 1879. It was located behind the 1843 building and faced Stockton Street. Instead of the more traditional stone, it was built of red pressed brick with stone trim. As already mentioned, it was called Lenox Library, but in later years it was simply referred to as the Seminary Library. Colloquially, the students dubbed it "The Brewery." The building was specifically designed to house books and other resources for daily use by students and staff. The older library was reserved for the more esoteric aspects of theological study.

John Frelinghuysen Hageman, Princeton historian of the 1870s, included a liberal sprinkling of personal comment in his narrative.

Lenox Library, Princeton Theological Seminary, N. J.

Publisher: McGown-Silsbee Litho Co., NY, Card No. 2578/2, 1435 * Manufacturer: McGown-Silsbee Litho Co., NY, Printed in Germany * Type: Colored, Bordered, Divided Back * Postmark: Not Used * Value Index: C

Although he was critical of the layout of the seminary campus, he flatly stated, "The buildings of the seminary are really more tasteful and substantial than those of the college."

There was anger and consternation in the Princeton community when the seminary razed the two old library buildings to make way for Speer Library (dedicated in 1958). Many residents were saddened to lose two outstanding examples of the town's architectural heritage.

It is interesting to note that a portrait painter was the inspiration for and the builder of Carnegie Lake. During his undergraduate days while rowing on the Delaware and Raritan Canal, Howard Russell Butler (Class of 1876) had dreamed of flooding the marshes behind the campus to form a lake. At the turn of the 20th century, while he was painting his first portrait of Andrew Carnegie, he interested the steel tycoon in underwriting the building of a lake. The completion of the lake was difficult and stormy. Princeton University President Woodrow Wilson wanted Mr. Carnegie to contribute to his preceptorial and graduate college plans. The gift of a lake led to his frequently quoted statement, "We went to

Washington St., Bridge over Carnegie Lake. PRINCETON, N. J.

Publisher: The Temme Co., Orange, NJ, Card No. 2076 * Manufacturer: The Temme Co., Orange, NJ, Made in Germany * Type: Colored, Divided Back * Postmark: Not Used * Value Index: D

Mr. Carnegie to ask bread and he gave us cake." Before the dream became reality, the cost of the lake was more than triple the estimated amount and the friendship between Mr. Carnegie and Mr. Butler had cooled.

The two roads which crossed the swamps had been carried on wooden bridges which had to be replaced. Fortunately for Princeton, the steel cantilever spans originally proposed were rejected by county officials. The beautiful bridge in the photograph continues to serve the community after more than 80 years. Someone in that horse and buggy age of dirt roads had the vision to provide a roadway over the lake wide enough to accommodate two adequate lanes of automobile traffic plus two sidewalks.

At Harrison Street, the second bridge over Lake Carnegie retained the same arches as at Washington Street (now Washington Road). In both design and capacity, however, it was more modest. As the picture shows, it was made of exposed steel construction, but the roadbed was narrower. When the automobile age arrived, the cars were barely able to pass in the two narrow lanes.

When "infrastructure" became a popular buzz word among governmental bodies, the county closed the bridge because it was unsafe. Engineering inspection revealed that replacement was necessary. This precipitated protracted negotiations among the governmental bodies involved. A particularly sticky issue concerned the aesthetics of the new bridge.

Harrison Street Bridge, Princeton, N. J.

Publisher: Christie Whiteman, Princeton, NJ * Manufacturer: Probably Curt Teich Co., Chicago, IL, or Brooklyn Post Card Co., Inc., New York, NY * Type: Colored, Divided Back * Postmark: September 12, 1914 * Value Index: D

Local government pushed to retain the graceful curve of the arches, and those paying the bills favored a more prosaic (and probably dull) design. For once, aesthetics won, but the victory probably added a year to the wait for the new bridge.

On the early postcards the illustrations were frequently identified as "Loch Carnegie" instead of "Lake Carnegie." Perhaps it was used in recognition of Andrew Carnegie's Scottish origins, but Carnegie was known to have referred to "The Loch." The gift was offered by Carnegie at a meeting in his home with Woodrow Wilson, President of Princeton University. Wilson immediately accepted the offer on behalf of the University. Ironically, the purpose for his visit had been to solicit funds for his new preceptorial system of undergraduate instruction. Carnegie's offer cut the ground out from under him. Carnegie never gave financial support to the preceptorial plan.

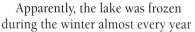

Publisher: McGown-Silsbee Litho Co., NY, Card No. 2578/6, 1439 * Manufacturer: McGown-Silsbee Litho Co., NY, Printed in Germany * Type: Colored, Divided Back * Postmark: Not Used * Value Index: D

Apparently, the lake was frozen during the winter almost every year and many people in the community enjoyed ice skating. In the 1960s a gym teacher in one of the local schools would assist the ice skaters when the ice was covered by new snow. He ordered the sixth, seventh, and eighth grade boys in his classes to report to the lake after school with their snow shovels. Most of the boys arrived, and space was cleared for skating. In recent years, good skating conditions have been rather rare. There are many theories for this phenomenon; one frequently heard is that pollutants in the water prevent the ice from forming.

The inspiration for the creation of Lake Carnegie was the students' longing to have a suitable body of water for rowing. Although the college acquired a lovely course for its crew races, the entire Princeton area has been the beneficiary. The development of Lake Carnegie has provided a facility for skating, recreational boating, fishing, trapping, and competitive sailing. These activities have given many hours of fun to the residents as well as the college community. For many years a boat house near the North end of the Washington Road bridge rented canoes ($.50 per hour). Nearby, a half-dozen white swans were usually waiting to be fed. Today, both the boat house and the swans are gone.

The island shown in the photograph was one of two created from

Publisher: Edw. J. Van Marter, Princeton, NJ, Card No. 2027/12, 8741 * Manufacturer: N. N., Distributed by E. W. Fausnaugh, Printed in Germany * Type: Colored, Divided Back * Postmark: Not Used * Value Index: D

the earth excavated to form the lake bed. The land to the east of Harrison Street bridge was also built up from the same material. Today, it is difficult to visualize that the excavating was almost entirely by hand with the assistance of horses, mules and dynamite. One local resident relates that his grandfather's first job was on this project. He earned $1.00 per day and he had to provide his own mule and cart.

This view of the "loch" shows two small shells practicing. The silhouette of tree limbs indicates that the time of year is late fall or early spring, but who are the three gentlemen with derbies standing at the left? Perhaps they were rowing coaches from the university.

Trees were important to Howard Russell Butler, whom Andrew Carnegie had insisted upon as the builder of Lake Carnegie. Although Butler was an artist rather than an engineer, he accepted the assignment. Before the excavating was done, he marked all of the trees which would overhang the lake so that they could be saved. The trees in the left foreground of the photograph were probably among them.

Loch Carnegie, Princeton, N. J.

Publisher: Edw. J. Van Marter, Princeton, NJ, Card No. 2027/4, 8733 * Manufacturer: N. N., Distributed by E. W. Fausnaugh, Printed in Germany * Type: Colored, Divided Back * Postmark: Not Used * Value Index: D

In the best Princeton tradition, the creation of a lake also created controversy in the town. It was argued that Stony Brook and the Millstone River would have insufficient water to keep the lake filled, that the mosquito population would multiply (despite the elimination of the swamps), and other comments. Most interesting was the cry of vandalism over the felling of so many trees. Eighty years later, the same cry was heard when it became necessary to remove trees in order to dredge the sediment from the Delaware and Raritan Canal. Butler's testy comment was, "Princeton is daft on the subject of trees—."

There are two errors on this postcard. In addition to the obvious misspelling of "Aqueduct," Delaware Canal usually referred to the canal which runs along the Pennsylvania side of the Delaware River. The Delaware and Raritan Canal (D & R) in New Jersey provided a water route from Bordentown to New Brunswick, which facilitated trade between New York and Philadelphia (roads were terrible and ocean routes were hazardous). The 22-mile feeder canal along the New Jersey bank of the Delaware River provided cheap transportation for the coal needed so desperately by the industrial cities.

The D & R Canal and the Camden and Amboy Railroad and Transportation Company were chartered at the same time, and

AQUADUCT, DELAWARE CANAL AND CARNEGIE LAKE, PRINCETON, N. J.

Publisher: Van Marter, Princeton, NJ, Card No. AD-5631 * Manufacturer: Curt Teich Co., Chicago, IL, "C. T. Doubletone," Made in U.S.A. * Type: Black and Sepia, Divided Back * Postmark: Not Used * Value Index: A

the two companies merged almost immediately. The colloquial identification was the "Joint Companies." The original railroad tracks were laid along the bank of the canal.

The photograph was taken after Lake Carnegie was created. Note that the levels of the lake, the canal, and the river varied by only a few feet. The fenced walkway on the far side of the canal is the tow path. The stone piers, where the fisherman sits, carried the tracks of the Camden and Amboy R. R. When the railroad route to New York was realigned after the Civil War, the tracks through Princeton were taken up.

The "Straight Turnpike" in this caption is now identified as U.S. Highway 1, and "Aqueduct" was a tiny village which had grown up around a mill whose history extended back to the 18th century. When the mill ceased operations about 1900, the village declined until only a few of the old buildings remained. The name came from the aqueduct which still carries the Delaware and Raritan Canal across the Millstone River. On the postcard, it is barely discernible in the background on the left, and the houses among the trees are in the hamlet. In acquiring the land for the lake, the purchase of the Aqueduct Mill was a keystone of the entire project. After bids for the excavation work had been received, it was discovered that the planned

LOCH CARNEGIE, PRINCETON, N. J., BETWEEN STRAIGHT TURNPIKE AND AQUEDUCT. SHOWING ONE OF ISLANDS IN LAKE

PUB BY VAN MARTER

Publisher: Van Marter, Princeton, NJ * Manufacturer: Not Indicated * Type: Black and White, Undivided Back * Postmark: Not Used * Value Index: E

level of the new lake would cause flooding along the Millstone River two miles upstream. Mr. Carnegie would not consider the purchase of additional land, and the lake level was reduced almost two feet to the level of the millpond. The fact that the mill had to maintain the river at that level was a valuable safeguard for the overall water level. Butler had to purchase thirty-one parcels of land to create the new lake. As might be expected, unclear titles, unknown owners, and profiteering created difficulties. He successfully assembled the package in three years. An unexpected benefit to the university was the land added to the campus. Some of the property owners would sell only their entire farms. Mr. Carnegie would buy only the needed acreage, but alumni and friends purchased the remainder of the land. One farm, renamed the Butler Tract, has been the university polo field and is the site of graduate housing built after World War II.

This view of the dam which created Lake Carnegie is from the strip of land which separates the lake from the D & R Canal. The crew races terminate a few hundred feet to the left of the photograph as the current near the dam can be dangerous. The old grist mill and village of Kingston are beyond the picture to the right. On the far side, the Princeton-Kingston Road runs parallel to the lake bank behind the house at the center. Today, although there are many more houses, particularly on the other side of the road, the view is remarkably unchanged. The trees effectively hide this small bit of Princeton's suburb.

Pub by Edw. G. van Marter

LOCH CARNEGIE, PRINCETON, N. J. DAM NEAR KINGSTON

Publisher: Edward G. van Marter, Princeton, NJ * Manufacturer: Not Indicated * Type: Colored, Divided Back * Postmark: Not Used * Value Index: C

Both the Kingston Flour Mill (without the cupola) and the bridge remain at the Princeton-Kingston border. The original mill was built in the 1750s on land purchased from the widow of a man bearing the fascinating name of Barefoot Brinson. It was burned during the Revolution, but a new mill ground grain until the last operator was drafted during World War II.

The 18th century wooden bridge over the Millstone River was destroyed after the Battle of Princeton by order of General Washington. Twenty-one years later, in 1798, the beautiful stone bridge shown in the photograph was built. In the 1960s, it, too, was threatened with destruction to make way for a modern four-lane replacement.

OLD GRIST MILL AT KINGSTON, N. J., JUST BELOW DAM OF LOCH CARNEGIE

PUB. BY VAN MARTER

Do you remember this place Carrie.

Publisher: Van Marter, Princeton, NJ * **Manufacturer:** Not Indicated * **Type:** Black and White, Undivided Back * **Postmark:** Not Used * **Value Index:** D

Fortunately, it was saved by the creation of a minipark which provides access to the recreational opportunities of the old canal. The new bridge was built over the stretch of water in the foreground of this picture. One casualty of the modernization is that this particular view is forever lost.

Commodore Robert Field Stockton, grandson of Richard Stockton, was the founding father of the Delaware and Raritan Canal. He convinced the legislature to grant the monopoly, also raised required funds during a national financial depression, and served as corporate president. Many people thought the project would be a losing proposition; the popular name for it was "Stockton's Folly."

The view in the photograph is downstream, looking toward Kingston. The railroad bridge mentioned in the caption continues in use by the "Dinky" train which carries passengers between Princeton and the main line of the railroad at Princeton Junction. Although it is now non-operative, it is a

VIEW OF CANAL FROM R. R. BRIDGE, PRINCETON, N. J.

Publisher: Christie Whiteman, Princeton, NJ * **Manufacturer:** Probably Curt Teich Co., Chicago, IL * **Type:** Colored, White Border, Divided Back * **Postmark:** Not Used * **Value Index:** E

swing bridge; it once pivoted on a massive steel cog mounted on a stone pillar next to the tow path. Walkers along the tow path can still see the mechanism.

A few hundred feet behind the photographer was a thriving little section of Princeton known merely as "The Basin." It was primarily a commercial center, but it also had a church, homes, a hotel, a tavern (of course), and a number of small businesses. Canal Street (now Alexander Street) was cut through from Mercer Street in the main part of town, because Commodore Stockton's headquarters were located in Ivy Hall (now owned by Trinity Episcopal Church). One writer has pointed out that until the Civil War began, the Basin was a busier place than the main town of Princeton. It was an active community until the Canal closed in the 1930s. Unfortunately, there are no known postcards of the basin area.

SCENE ON THE CANAL, PRINCETON, N. J.

Publisher: Christie Whiteman, Princeton, NJ * Manufacturer: Probably Curt Teich Co., Chicago, IL * Type: Colored, White Border, Divided Back * Postmark: Not Used * Value Index: E

DELAWARE & RARITAN CANAL, BELOW KINGSTON, AND LOCH CARNEGIE, N. J.

PUB. BY VAN MARTER

Publisher: Van Marter, Princeton, NJ * Manufacturer: Not Indicated * Type: Blue and White, Brown Undivided Back * Postmark: Not Used * Value Index: B

This scene is probably the curve east of Washington Road. Understandably, there are no trees along the tow path to interfere with the tow ropes. When the canal was dredged to improve the water flow, it was necessary to remove some of the trees, bushes, etc., which had grown along the banks in the 50 years since the canal closed. The anguished cry then was to "restore" the canal to its original beauty. This picture clearly shows the original appearance.

The canal engineer, Canvass White, was also the builder of the Erie Canal. Today, it is difficult to comprehend that 60 miles of canal were dug with pick and shovel with the assistance of horse-drawn scoops and scrapers. Hundreds of laborers, mostly Irish, did the digging and the stonework. Despite the occurrence of a cholera epidemic, the work was completed in four years. Unfortunately, Mr. White did not live to see his canal completed. He died in St. Petersburg, Florida, and his body was returned to Princeton for interment in Princeton Cemetery.

The postcard illustrated is the only one known to the author of the Princeton segment of the canal which shows a vessel of any type. That seems odd, because the Delaware & Raritan (D & R) Canal rivalled the Erie Canal in tonnage shipped; it was a heavily used waterway. However, the photographs may have been taken on a Sunday, because state Blue Laws prohibited freight transportation on that day.

Note that the vessel is a power boat. As on other canals, mules were the principal source of power, but a unique feature of the D & R Canal was that it was constructed to accommodate steam-powered vessels. Commodore Stockton had a screw-driven tug built in Europe. It was the first iron vessel to cross the Atlantic Ocean and was the first commercially successful propeller-driven vessel in this country. The tug towed barges on the canal for thirty years.

In the declining years of canal traffic, private yachts frequented the Canal, particularly in the fall and spring for their trek to Florida. Traveling through the canal cut out 200 miles of rough and risky ocean travel. There are also many tales about Princeton University alumni parking their yachts at the Basin when they came from New York to attend a football game.

As might be expected, the men working on the canal were a rough and tumble group and the boats seemed to have been fair game for the residents along the route. Mischievous boys would swim under water to a barge loaded with watermelons, pull one or more melons from the stack, the stack would collapse into the water, and the boys could swim off with their booty. Enterprising residents along the banks lined up bottles on their fences. As coal barges floated by the operators did the natural thing of throwing pieces of coal at the bottles. The residents had their coal supply for the winter. Life along the canal was not placid.

Publisher: Not Indicated * Manufacturer: Not Indicated * Type: Photograph (EKC) * Postmark: Not Used * Value Index: C

This "Bird's Eye View of Princeton University" was probably photographed from Holder Tower at the same time as the "Bird's Eye View of Princeton" on page 21. As you look over the roof of Holder Hall in the foreground, the white stucco of First Presbyterian Church and stone-turreted Alexander Hall dominate the scene. Shortly after the College of New Jersey moved to Princeton in 1756, the first of three church buildings was constructed on this site. For the first half-century or more, the President of the College (always a Presbyterian Minister) served as pastor of the church. In return, the church sanctuary was used for commencement exercises and other convocations. As enrollments grew after the Civil War, the need for a larger assembly room grew apace; this need was met by the construction of Alexander Hall in 1892.

Just over the roof of the church can be seen the John Maclean House, originally built as the residence for the President of the College. To the south (right) are Stanhope Hall, Reunion Hall, and West College. Although Stanhope Hall (built in 1803) is the third oldest building on the campus, it has never been a popular postcard subject. A modest building in size, it originally was called the Library, although it also housed study halls and the Whig and Clio Literary Societies. Over the years, it use gradually changed to house administrative functions, and when this picture was taken, its was the home of the university offices. Reunion Hall (built in 1870) was a five-floor dormitory razed in the 1960s as a fire hazard. West College (built in 1836) was a dormitory until the 1960s, when it was converted to undergraduate administrative offices.

In the center of the picture, the cupola of Nassau Hall (1756) is easily discerned. On the horizon, at the left, can be seen the square tower of the John C. Green School of Science (1874) which burned down in 1928. Just to the right of Nassau Hall is the slender spire of Marquand Chapel, which was destroyed by fire in 1920. By itself, at the far right, is the original Art Museum which served the University from the 1880s to the 1960s when it was replaced.

Color versions of the bird's eye view were also published by McGown-Silsbee Litho Co., printed in Germany.

Nassau St., front of Campus, Princeton Univ

Publisher: Van Marter, Princeton, NJ * Manufacturer: N. N., distributed by E. W. Fausnaugh, Printed in Germany * Type: Colored, Divided Back * Postmark: Not Used * Value Index: C

This view of Nassau Street looking east from Witherspoon Street describes, with a single picture, the sleepy country village of Princeton at the beginning of the 20th century. When was the last time you could stand on this spot at high noon and see only a single automobile for several blocks, and not a pedestrian in sight? Today, it might be difficult to comprehend that at one time, Princeton University was essentially closed down after the spring graduation. Business establishments closed for the summer months, and there was a mass exodus of residents to the seashore, Maine, and other vacation spots. Priest's Drug Store opened a store in Bay Head, New Jersey, during the hot months.

At the right of the picture is the FitzRandolph Gateway, the imposing main entrance to the campus of Princeton University. Erected in 1905, it was the gift of a descendant of Nathaniel FitzRandolph, a prime mover in enticing the College of New Jersey to move to Princeton, and the donor of the four-and-one-half acres on which Nassau Hall and Maclean House stand. The 19th century fence replaced by the gateway was moved to the Second Presbyterian Church (now the Nassau Christian Center). In the 1960s the wrought iron fence was moved once more; it now embellishes a home at 12 Morven Place.

Publisher: E.J. Van Marter, Princeton, NJ * Manufacturer: Printed in Germany * Type: Colored, Undivided Back *
Postmark: Not Used * Value Index: D

Publisher: Not Indicated * Manufacturer: Not Indicated * Type: Photograph,
Divided Back * Postmark: Not Used * Value Index: C

The FitzRandolph Gateway appropriately frames the view of Nassau Hall's cupola and the front campus. The urns on the two smaller columns are similar to the urns which decorated the college's first wall. The imperial (and imperious) eagles which glare at each other across the center gate are similar to those which adorned New York City's spectacular Pennsylvania Railroad Station (razed in the 1960s).

Postcards reveal the subtleties of the gateway's tradition and symbolism. Although the illustration is identified as the "Main Entrance," the early postcards always show the three sets of gates closed. Also, examination under a magnifying glass indicates that they were not in daily use as entrances. On later postcards, the smaller gates on each side are open, and the center is closed. This was the period when the center gate was opened only for the alumni parade at commencement or for an especially distinguished visitor, such as a President of the United States. In the 1960s the center gate was thrown open permanently and the side gates were closed to show the community and the world that they are welcome to Princeton University. Also, the paths leading to the side gates have been removed.

This photograph clearly shows the Nassau Hall tower as it was seen through the narrow walkway between the university offices (now Stanhope Hall) and Reunion Hall (razed in 1965).

A close look at the path in the foreground reveals that a student in cap and gown is running towards the photographer. As mentioned above, the old Postcards rarely included any people, especially unposed. The questions raised here are intriguing. Why is he running? Why is he wearing a cap and gown? Is he late for some sort of convocation in Alexander Hall (behind the photographer), such as graduation? If the latter, would it have been held at 2:25 P.M.? We will never know the answers to these questions.

For over 230 years, the ringing of a bell in the cupola has assisted both students and townspeople to meet their daily schedules. Early records of the college relate numerous instances when students broke into the belfry at night to ring the bell. Usually it was a feature of a student riot or rebellion. After the Civil War, an annual ritualistic prank was the theft of the bell clapper. The university kept an ample supply of spares on hand to minimize the effect on the bell schedule. When Senator Bill Bradley played his last game on the campus at the close of his brilliant All-American basketball career, a grateful student body presented him with a mounted clapper as a memento of his contribution to the athletic program.

At the outbreak of the Civil War, a spectacular incident occurred at the tower. In Princeton, patriotic fervor ran high for both North and South, and preference was shown by flying appropriate colors. Because of the large number of southern students, the college banned the display of any flag. A contemporary writer commented that "The Professors were guarded in their speech and sought at first to repress all patriotic demonstrations among the students, whether loyal or disloyal." He went on to say that Captain John H. Margerum climbed to the top of the dome and, -"amid the enthusiastic cheers of the students,—" restored the Stars and Stripes to the weather vane. In gratitude, the students presented him with a brace of pistols. This event is memorialized by a bronze plaque on Captain Margerum's grave in the Princeton Cemetery.

Nassau Hall, Princeton University Erected 1756.

Publisher: Edw. J. Van Marter, Princeton, NJ, Card No. 2027/8, 8737 *
Manufacturer: N. N., Distributed by E. W. Fausnaugh, Printed in Germany *
Type: Colored, Divided Back * Postmark: Not Used * Value Index: C

Nassau Hall or North College, Princeton, N. J.

Publisher: American News Company, NY, Leipzig, Berlin and Dresden, Card No. C3810, 120483 * Manufacturer: American
News Co., NY, Leipzig, Berlin, Germany * Type: Colored, Divided Back * Postmark: Not Used * Value Index: D

This view of "Old North" shows the massive construction of the building. Locally quarried stone was used, and the walls are more than two feet thick. Undoubtedly, this is a major factor in it having stood for almost 250 years. It was occupied and ravaged by both British and Colonial troops during the Revolution, and it has survived two major fires. Above all, it survived the rebellions and riots of the students. In the early decades, repressive rules and a "Big Brother" type of supervision were considered necessary to develop character. The rigid 5 A.M. to 9 P.M. schedule prescribed for the students included only about three hours of discretionary time. Games and athletics were deemed to be "a frivolity," and a responsibility of the tutors was to report any infraction of the rules, such as the ban on sleigh-riding. Reaction to boredom and oppression was sometimes violent. "Crackers" (homemade explosive devices), pistols, and horns were popular noisemakers when the students rebelled and/or rioted. During the "Great Rebellion of 1807," Nassau Hall was barricaded, and armed students repelled the faculty and townspeople who attempted to limit damage to the building. As a result, seventy students were expelled, and a list of their names was sent to other colleges requesting that the expelled students be denied admission. Only the University of Pennsylvania refused to honor the blacklist. A few years later, Nassau Hall was endangered once more when a "cracker" fashioned from a hollow log was detonated behind the main entrance. The explosion cracked the walls from the bottom to the top of the building and shattered many of the windows. Fortunately, no one was injured.

Close examination of this photograph shows that the picture was taken before 1911. The main entrance is guarded by a pair of lions which had been given by Woodrow Wilson's class in 1879. After the official adoption of the tiger as a school symbol, the class gave the pair of bronze tigers in 1911. The lions were moved to Class of '79 Hall, where they looked down Prospect Street. At some time during the World War II or post-war era they were removed. Fortunately, an alumnus who has retired to Princeton has located them so that they can be restored to the campus.

Nassau Hall, which used to be affectionately called "Old North," was the original building for the College of New Jersey when it moved to Princeton in 1756. It was the largest stone building in the thirteen colonies. Imagine the impact it must have had on travellers passing through the sparsely settled countryside when they saw it standing on a treeless plain at the crest of the ridge.

A favorite tale concerns the naming of the building. Jonathan Belcher, Governor of the Province of New Jersey, had been a powerful influence in clarifying the legal status of the struggling new institution, in raising money, and in selecting Princeton as the site for the school. When the trustees offered to name the new building for him, the governor modestly declined the honor and recommended the name "Nassau Hall" in honor of King William III, Prince of Orange and Nassau. Princetonians have been grateful ever since; somehow, "Belcher Hall" does not have quite the appropriate academic ring to it.

The building was designed to house all of the college functions. According to one contemporary source, "it would accommodate 147 students, based on a calculation of three students to a chamber. These chambers were twenty feet square, with two large closets, and a window in each for retirement." The writer did not explain where the third student would retire. There was also an "elegant hall of genteel workmanship" with a gallery and a stage. In that stern Presbyterian era, eyebrows must have been raised to see "A small, though exceeding good organ" in the hall. A library of 1,200 volumes was on the second floor, and in the basement were "A commodious dining hall," kitchen and steward's apartments. Interestingly, this particular source did not mention that the tutors lived among (and spied on) the students, nor did he mention any of the classroom facilities.

Publisher: Not Indicated, Card No. 63843 * Manufacturer: Not Indicated * Type: Colored, Divided Back * Postmark: Not Used * Value Index: D

Publisher: W. C. Sinclair, Princeton, NJ, Card No. B7837 * Manufacturer: American News Co., NY, Leipzig, Berlin, Made in Germany * Type: Black and White, Divided Back * Postmark: Not Used * Value Index: E

This view looking across Cannon Green shows the back of Nassau Hall. The extension of the building which dominates the center of the picture was originally less than one-half of its present depth. In the early days of the college, it was the prayer hall, but after the second great fire, it was enlarged and converted to the college library. Later, it served as a museum. Finally, in 1906, it was remodeled in the image of the British House of Commons for use as the Faculty Room.

The Battle of Princeton in 1777 ended at this spot, but the colonial artillery had left its mark. A portrait of King George II in the prayer hall was decapitated by a cannon ball, and another scarred the wall at the left of the extension. Later, the frame for the destroyed picture was recycled; it now contains Charles Willson Peale's portrait of General George Washington. On the wall, the university carefully keeps the ivy trimmed so that visitors may see the evidence left by the Revolutionary battle.

Although Nassau Hall had not yet been fully repaired from the destruction of the Revolution, in 1783 the Continental Congress met for four months in the library, which was then located on the second floor at the front of the building. Much has been written about the glittering social galas and important political events, but imagine the impact on a rural hamlet of a few hundred souls when the entire government of the new country dropped in for the summer! Because Congress was fleeing from its own army, there was no time for preparation, housing varied between inadequate and nonexistent, and supplies of all kinds were quickly exhausted. Profiteering was rampant, and to exacerbate the situation, the temperature was suffocatingly hot. The visitors grumbled about the primitive living conditions and were glad to return to the amenities of the city. Princeton was not a tourist attraction in those days.

Over the years many buildings on the campus have been renamed, either officially by the university trustees or unofficially from everyday usage. The house shown on the postcard was built concurrently with Nassau Hall as the residence for the president of the college. In November 1756, President Aaron Burr, Sr., moved in with his wife, Esther, his daughter, Sarah, and his infant son, Aaron, Jr.. Subsequent presidents lived there until 1878 when the more imposing Prospect was given to the college. The building then acquired the name of Dean's House, because the deans of the faculty lived there until 1967, when it was converted for the Alumni Council's use. It has been officially renamed John Maclean House in honor of the president who founded the Alumni Council.

Tradition tells us that the two old sycamore trees which stand on the front lawn were planted in 1766 to celebrate the repeal of the British Stamp Tax. As an apocryphal story, it is appealing, however, one historian said, "But unless one ascribe to the trustees the gift of prophecy the claim can have no justification." The trees had been ordered a year before the repeal.

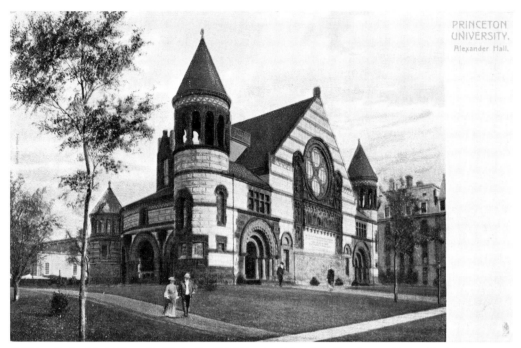

Publisher: Raphael Tuck & Sons, Card Series No. 2069 "Princeton University" * Manufacturer: Raphael Tuck & Sons, London, England * Type: Colored, Undivided Back * Postmark: Not Used * Value Index: E

Publisher: The Valentine & Sons Publishing Co. Ltd., NY, Card No. 202,190 * Manufacturer: The Valentine & Sons Publishing Co. Ltd., NY, Printed in Great Britain * Type: Colored, Undivided Back * Postmark: Not Used * Value Index: D

As we begin a serpentine tour to the other buildings on the main university campus, Alexander Hall is the first stop. For over a century, commencements and other major convocations were held in the First Presbyterian Church. By the close of the 19th century, the church sanctuary had become inadequate. The completion of Alexander Hall in 1892 solved the problem; the 1500 seats in the new hall could accommodate the entire student body and the faculty with room to spare. Commencement was held here until 1922, when the growth of the student body forced relocation of the ceremony to the campus in front of Nassau Hall. After Marquand Chapel burned, Sunday services were conducted here while the present chapel was under construction.

The Romanesque architectural style was a sharp break from the more austere styles of other buildings on the campus. Over the years, popular opinion concerning the building has ebbed and flowed. For example, shortly after it was completed, it was described as a handsome structure of brownstone and granite. Forty years later, it was called "over-ornate, heavy and ill-proportioned," but two decades after that, a critic said it is "vigorous, consistent, and refined." One fact is certain; individual opinions of the hall's beauty are seldom neutral.

This photograph shows the rear of the building. At the left, the back wall of the First Presbyterian Church is visible, and Reunion Hall can be seen at the right. The rose window midway between the two towers overlooks the stage. Originally, it could be seen from every seat in the auditorium.

As the photograph clearly shows, the original stage was designed for formal meetings. The marble panels at the front match the wall behind the pew-like semicircular ranks of seats. The three mosaics which dominate the background are scenes from the legends of Homer. Above, but not shown in this picture, is the beautiful rose window. You will note from the foreground that the audience sat on wooden benches. This was also true for the balcony.

In 1984, Alexander Hall had a major remodeling, and the hall was dedicated as Richardson Auditorium. The stage has been extended (the formal seats and rostrum had been eliminated years before), the auditorium is now air conditioned, the acoustics have been improved, and comfortable seating has replaced the hard wooden benches. The community especially benefits from the modernization, because it has provided opportunities for public concerts and other cultural events. If one were to cavil at any aspect of the present auditorium, it is the fact that the acoustical treatment blocks the view of the rose window, the principal feature of the original design. Perhaps this can be justified by the fact that the major events are held in the evening when the beauty of the window cannot be enjoyed.

As mentioned elsewhere, the early postcards of Holder Tower usually identified it as Sage Tower in recognition of the donor, Mrs. Russell Sage. It is a close copy of a tower at England's Canterbury Cathedral. The dormitories in the picture are Holder Hall (1910), and a photograph taken from the same spot today would look essentially the same. When excavation was underway prior to construction, 32 unmarked graves of the old FitzRandolph family graveyard were uncovered. The remains were carefully boxed and were reinterred under an arch of the new hall. They are memorialized on a plaque which pays tribute to "Nathaniel FitzRandolph the generous giver of the land upon which the original buildings of this university were erected." Before this complex

Publisher: Princeton University Store, Princeton, NJ, Card No. AA6109 * Manufacturer: American News Co., NY, Leipzig, Dresden, Berlin, "Steeldrucktone," Made in Germany * Type: Black and Sepia, Divided Back * Postmark: Not Used * Value Index: D

could be built, it was necessary to acquire the approximately one-half dozen private homes on Nassau Street between the First Presbyterian Church and University Hall on the corner of Railroad Avenue (now University Place). Twenty-three years were required to obtain titles to the properties. In true Princeton tradition, the land was finally cleared in the summer of 1909 by moving the last three houses to Greenholm and Cleveland Lane. The buildings had to be moved in seven sections; what an exciting event it must have been in the village during the summer doldrums!

The construction of Madison Hall in 1916 on the site of the old University Hall represented a major step towards resolving the long-standing problems of feeding the college students. Originally, spartan meals were served in the basement of Nassau Hall, and complaints about the food were frequent. Students were forbidden to supplement their diet with purchases from the townspeople, a rule impossible to enforce. It was not uncommon for them to steal local chickens or turkeys and cook them over the fire which heated their rooms. In the 19th century, the refectories were in buildings separate from Nassau Hall. In fact, one was located off the campus in a ramshackle house on William Street. By the 1840s, students were per-

Publisher: Not Indicated * Manufacturer: Not Indicated * Type: Photograph, Divided Back * Postmark: Not Used * Value Index: C

mitted to take meals in the village; apparently, the college was unable to compete. The refectory was closed down in 1856. Efforts to restore campus food services were unsuccessful until commons were established in University Hall at the beginning of the 20th century. The new Madison Hall provided five dining rooms which were supplied by a central kitchen.

In the early days, student objections to the meals were emphatically expressed. A common device was to shuffle their feet at the table. Of course, anyone detected in this unruly behavior was subject to severe punishment. A more pointed protest was when the students picked up the table covers with the dishes of food on them and threw them out of the windows.

The cryptic message on this postcard is especially thought-provoking when one considers that it was mailed from an all-male university to a certain Miss in Syracuse, New York. Each reader develops his or her own scenario leading up to such an emotional comment. Let your imagination run free; the truth will never be known.

Aside from Nassau Hall, the University Hotel was the most imposing, or perhaps over-powering structure in Princeton when it was built in 1875 at the southeast corner of Nassau Street and Railroad Avenue (University Place). At one time it housed the local bank, the telegraph office (important in the pre-telephone era), and a "tonsorial parlor" (barber shop).

Publisher: Not Indicated * Manufacturer: Not Indicated * Type: Photograph, Undivided Back * Postmark: October 26, 1907 * Value Index: A

For the students, it was important as the site for dances and other social events. Because the hotel was never profitable, it passed into the hands of the college in 1883 and was renamed University Hall for use as a dormitory and commons. It was also the first home of the Nassau Club of Princeton, which celebrated its centennial in 1989. The building was demolished in 1916 to make way for the construction of Madison Hall.

Next to the hall, at the lower left, the former home of Arnold Guyot is visible. Guyot was the college's first Professor of Geology and Geography, and Guyot Hall is named for this world-renowned scholar. His home was famous for its beautiful gardens. The house was moved to Greenholm in the multiple house-moving of 1909.

This photograph clearly shows the steps leading from the railroad station through Blair Tower to the campus. Note the edge of the train platform at the lower left and the double tracks. Service to Princeton Junction was frequent and reliable in those days before cars and buses. As most of the visitors arrived by train, the steps and Blair Tower provided a spectacular introduction to the University.

Stafford Little Hall was the second Collegiate Gothic dormitory. Following the example of Blair Hall it extended along what was the western boundary line of the campus. Expansion to University Place was not possible until the railroad station was moved to its present location.

The students living in this dormitory must also have endured the

Blair and Little Hall, Princeton University.

Publisher: Van Marter, Princeton, NJ, Card No. 2489/18 5406 * Manufacturer: Printed in Germany * Type: Colored, Divided Back * Postmark: Not Used * Value Index: D

locomotive smoke and fumes, although probably not as severely as those in Blair Hall where the engines waited below their windows at the end of the tracks.

Publisher: Illustrated Postal Card Co., NY, Card No. 99.-4 * Manufacturer: Illustrated Postal Card Co., NY, Germany * Type: Colored, Undivided Back * Postmark: November 5, 1906 * Value Index: E

Publisher: Van Marter, Princeton, NJ, Card No. 2489/13 5401 * Manufacturer: Printed in Germany * Type: Colored, Divided Back * Postmark: Not Used * Value Index: D

Oddly enough, although the Halstead Observatory was a unique structure on the Princeton Campus, only a few postcards showing it were published. The one illustrated here is the most common version, but it is unusual in some respects. It is the only postcard which shows a night scene. As mentioned elsewhere, it was a common practice to "improve" the original picture. In this instance, lighted windows and the spatter of stars were added by an artist. Although the art work is crude, the night scene is appropriate for the subject, and the overall result is a very attractive postcard.

This particular postcard was mailed to Dolington, a hamlet just outside of Yardley in Bucks County, Pennsylvania. The postmark shows that it was mailed from Trenton, New Jersey, at 6 P.M. on November 5, 1906, and a second cancellation records that it was received in Dolington in the morning of November 6. For some unknown reason, it had been missent to the next town, Taylorsville (now Washington Crossing, Pennsylvania), where a third cancellation shows that it had been received at 8 A.M. on the same day. We consider 1906 to be in the horse and buggy era, we might wonder whether our modern technology can improve on that mail service.

Unlike many of the campus buildings, the need for an observatory was not quickly satisfied. Although the college was urged to build the structure for its Astronomy Department as early as 1848, it did not become a reality until 1869. Even then, the telescope was not added for another fifteen years! When the Halstead Observatory was razed in the 1930s to make way for the building of Joline Hall, the stones were reused to build the FitzRandolph Observatory which still stands near Lake Carnegie.

The university's plan for developing the corner of the main campus west of the First Presbyterian Church and Alexander Hall began to take tangible shape in 1909. The old Gymnasium (1869) was torn down and Campbell Hall, an L-shaped dormitory, was built midway between Alexander Hall and the Halstead Observatory. The construction of Holder (1910), Hamilton (1911) and Madison (1916) Halls quickly followed, but the overall plan was not fully completed until 1932, when Joline Hall replaced the old Halstead Observatory.

Although the plan required one-third of a century to complete, the funding for the first dormitory in that segment of the campus must hold the record for raising money. At the 30th reunion dinner for the Class of 1877, Moses Taylor Pyne pointed out the need for dormitories and reminded his classmates that other classes had already made significant contributions to this particular cause. This triggered a spontaneous auction in which the men vied with each other to pledge contributions toward the erection of a new dormitory. In less than one hour, almost eighty percent of the required amount was pledged, and the balance of the money was raised from other class members. Two years later, the new dormitory was occupied.

The new building was named for John Alexander Campbell, a prominent Trenton banker and industrialist. Although the Class of 1877 had many distinguished members, Mr. Campbell was elected its president in his freshman year and continued in that post for 50 years after graduation.

For a quarter of a century after its erection in 1897, Blair Hall was the main campus entrance on the western border. On the other side of the archway is a flight of steps which led down to the Pennsylvania Railroad Station, then located near where the University Store now stands. From the beginning, the tower suites of rooms were coveted by the students. They were not always the most pleasant, however, until the station was relocated down the hill. The coal-burning locomotives "parked" at the foot of Blair steps, and the rooms above were the beneficiaries of the soot and fumes. In 1896 the trustees decreed that the Collegiate Gothic style of architecture was to be standard for new buildings. Dean Andrew

7265. BLAIR HALL, PRINCETON UNIVERSITY, PRINCETON, N. J.

Publisher: Detroit Photographic Co., Copyright 1903, Card No. 7265 * Manufacturer: Detroit Photographic Co. * Type: Colored, White Border, Undivided Back * Postmark: Not Used * Value Index: E

West, father of the graduate school, had seen examples at Bryn Mawr College and the University of Pennsylvania. He convinced Moses Taylor Pyne, Chairman of the Buildings and Grounds Committee, that it was a fitting architectural style for Princeton; Blair Hall was the first and foremost example. As one author said "experimentation ceased;" Collegiate Gothic ruled the building program for the next half century. The donor, John Insley Blair, was a self-made man in the Horatio Alger tradition. At age eleven, he left school to work in a country store. Before he was thirty, he owned a small empire of stores and flour mills. He then branched out into iron mining and railroads, and it was said that he owned more miles of railroad than anyone in the world. He was conscientious in sharing his wealth. Besides his gifts to the college, he was a benefactor of Blair Academy in Blairstown, New Jersey, and he helped to found over 100 Presbyterian churches.

This 1900 picture of Stafford Little Hall (1899 and 1901), framed between the corners of Witherspoon and Blair Halls, was taken before the dormitory was completed. At the right, the passenger platform of the railroad station is visible. Beyond that, trees and residences can be seen through the small plume of smoke. This area was the western edge of the campus.

Henry Stafford Little, Class of 1844, was another one of the loyal, active, and generous individuals who have characterized the Princeton University alumni. He was president of a railroad, presided over the New Jersey Senate for several years, and

7266. STAFFORD LITTLE HALL, PRINCETON UNIVERSITY.

Publisher: Detroit Photographic Co., Copyright 1900, Card No. 7266 * Manufacturer: Detroit Photographic Co. * Type: Colored, White Border, Undivided Back * Postmark: * Value Index: C

served the University as a trustee. After Grover Cleveland retired in Princeton, Mr. Little endowed a lectureship with the stipulation that Mr. Cleveland should be its incumbent during his lifetime. Many years later, Albert Einstein delivered five Stafford Little lectures on the Theory of Relativity. The resultant book was the first Einstein volume to be published in the United States.

Witherspoon Hall (1877) was the first residential building to deviate from the severe architecture of older dormitories such as West College. In its day, it was considered to be the most beautiful and luxurious dormitory in the country, but over the years, the reviews have been less effusive. One critic termed it "almost a catalogue of High Victorian vices and virtues." Another stated that it "illustrates perfectly the lack of systematic planning in architectural development of the campus." An alumnus, reminiscing many years later, commented that "Witherspoon Hall, with sixty suites and nary a bathroom, still made architects of other colleges green with envy."

Publisher: A. C. Bosselman & Co., NY, Card No. 885 * Manufacturer: Made in Germany * Type: Colored, Undivided Back * Postmark: Not Used * Value Index: E

The dormitory was composed of forty single rooms plus a number of suites consisting of two bedrooms and a study. Regardless of architectural opinion, it became the most popular housing on the campus. One adjective used was "Aristocratic," because it was deemed to be the home for the wealthier students. An early resident, however, was Woodrow Wilson, Class of 1879, who was the son of a Presbyterian minister.

This photograph of Witherspoon and Stafford Little Halls, with a corner of Blair Hall at the left, shows how thoroughly Witherspoon Hall dominated this corner of the campus. Five stories high, massively built, and situated on relatively high ground, the sprawling dormitories on lower ground were somewhat dwarfed in comparison. Notice how the steps coming down from behind Blair Hall to the walkway entrance columns drew the three buildings together. The fence undoubtedly served to prevent students from taking shortcuts to the railroad station.

Stafford Little Hall holds the distinction of being the first dormitory built with bathrooms. One author quoted the Alumni Weekly as follows: "There are to be

Publisher: Not Indicated * Manufacturer: Not Indicated * Type: Photograph, Divided Back * Postmark: Not Used * Value Index: B

baths in the new Little Hall! This will be astonishing news to many old graduates, alarming news to certain older graduates, who shook their heads once upon a time when bathrooms were put in—Reunion Hall and who said, `I told you so,' when an epidemic of typhoid broke out—Some of the trustees, it is said, have never believed in baths since. In dormitories, that is."

The erection of Brokaw Memorial Hall in 1892 was the first step towards moving the physical education facilities to the southwestern segment of the campus. Its principal feature was the college's first swimming pool, 100 by 25 feet. Access to the building was easy and direct; the path at the west end of Nassau Hall ran straight from Nassau Street to the arch of Brokaw Hall. Nearby were 22 tennis courts and Brokaw Field, which contained three baseball diamonds. The new gymnasium was added to the western end of the building in 1903.

BROKAW HALL, PRINCETON UNIVERSITY, PRINCETON, N. J.

Publisher: Not Indicated * Manufacturer: Not Indicated * Type: Black and White, Divided Back * Postmark: Not Used * Value Index: C

As president, Dr. McCosh broke with his predecessors, who had been luke-warm at best toward any form of athletics. He was a firm believer in "A sound mind in a sound body." Princeton's participation in organized inter-collegiate athletics dates from his era, and the extensive program of physical education and intermural sports can trace its origins to that great president.

Brokaw Hall was a fitting memorial to Frederick Brokaw, who lost his life in 1891 while attempting to save a drowning girl. He was a member of the baseball team and would have graduated in 1892.

When this Collegiate Gothic gymnasium was opened in 1903, it joined Blair and Stafford Little Halls to clearly delineate the Western boundary of the campus. Funds for its construction were raised by popular subscription, and one gift in particular was especially appreciated. Jimmie Johnson, campus vendor of fruit and candy, an escaped slave whose freedom had been purchased by the students, contributed a gift of one dollar. Unlike most of the buildings on the campus it was not named for a major donor. It was simply called "University Gymnasium," which was quickly shortened by usage to "Gymnasium." In its day, it was the largest structure of its kind in the country.

During World War II, after forty years of service to the

GYMNASIUM, PRINCETON UNIVERSITY, PRINCETON, N. J.

Publisher: A. C. Bosselman & Co., NY, Card No. 880 * Manufacturer: Made in Germany * Type: Colored, Undivided Back * Postmark: Not Used * Value Index: E

University, an early morning fire completely destroyed the building and its contents. Fortunately, the fire fighters were able to prevent it from spreading to nearby dormitories. Alumni and friends quickly rallied their forces; in less than three years, money was raised and Dillon Gymnasium was built and opened in 1947.

As mentioned elsewhere, interior scenes were seldom shown on early postcards. Despite this fact the next four illustrations show the interior of the gymnasium building. They are probably a reflection of the tremendous interest which must have been generated in the student body by this magnificent new facility. One can imagine the students' reaction to moving from a tiny, cramped, dingy, and poorly ventilated building to the largest gymnasium in the country with adequate facilities for all of the indoor sports, plus locker rooms and showers for the students.

The Trophy Room was located in the front section of the building. The banner suspended from the balcony railing was a memento of the Sesquicentennial Celebration of 1896 when the College of New

Jersey officially adopted the name of Princeton University. In the same section were located the offices for the hygiene and physical education staff, as well as physical examination rooms and facilities for fencing, boxing, and wrestling.

Publisher: Van Marter, Princeton, NJ, Card No. 2489/15, 5403 * Manufacturer: Printed in Germany * Type: Colored, Divided Back * Postmark: Not Used * Value Index: D

As this postcard clearly shows, the Trophy Room was beautifully paneled and trimmed in English Oak. It was a spectacular entrance for a gymnasium. Previously, the University's "Precious collection of trophies" had been housed in the Osborn Field House (now the Third World Center) on the corner of Olden Street and Prospect Avenue. Most of the trophies were transferred to the new Trophy Room, and they were destroyed in the disastrous 1944 fire.

As so often happens after such a major disaster, an apocryphal story came out of the gymnasium holocaust. It has been said that melted remains of the trophies were salvaged from the ruins and the metal was

TROPHY ROOM, GYMNASIUM, PRINCETON UNIVERSITY, PRINCETON, N. J.

Publisher: C. E. Van Marter, Princeton, NJ, Card No. A-86314 * Manufacturer: Curt Teich Co., Chicago, IL, "C. T. American Art," Made in U.S.A. * Type: Colored, White Border, Divided Back * Postmark: Not Used * Value Index: C

incorporated into the casting of the tiger which crouches at the entrance to Palmer Square. Although of doubtful authenticity, it is an ingenious bit of folklore.

The view of the main section of the gymnasium clearly shows its immense size. The massive buttressed stone walls were the sole support of the roof so that there was an unobstructed room 166 feet in length and 101 feet wide. Notice the small appearance of the gymnastic apparatus at the end of the room. Suspended from the walls was a running track. Approximately ten laps around the track was supposed to represented a run of one mile. Note the numerous large windows. Major criticisms of the old Bonner-Marquand Gymnasium were poor lighting and inadequate ventilation. Obviously, the architects addressed those problems in the new building.

INTERIOR OF GYMNASIUM, PRINCETON, N. J.

Publisher: Probably Christie Whiteman, Princeton, NJ * Manufacturer: Probably Curt Teich Co., Chicago, IL * Type: Colored, White Border, Divided Back * Postmark: Not Used * Value Index: E

Like most stone buildings of that period, the interior structure was primarily wood. This picture shows thousands of square feet of oak flooring and wood panelling, and that does not include the hidden structure. In the fire, the incredible heat melted and twisted the steel beams into a surreal pile of metal pretzels.

When the new gymnasium was built in 1902-03, it was connected to the Brokaw Memorial Building, which contained the swimming pool. By today's standards, the pool seems small, but at the turn of the century, indoor pools of any size were uncommon. A handbook published at that time describes it as a "Porcelain swimming pool"! The black panels at the end and sides of the pool are actually long radiators mounted on the wall. Since the building was heated by steam, you can be sure that the swimmers kept a respectful distance between themselves and the wall.

Shortly after the completion of the new gymnasium, the University Power Company (wholly owned by Princeton University) built a power plant

SWIMMING POOL, PRINCETON, N. J.

Publisher: Probably Christie Whiteman, Princeton, NJ * Manufacturer: Probably Curt Teich Co., Chicago, IL * Type: Colored, White Border, Divided Back * Postmark: Not Used * Value Index: E

which stretched along the backs of Brokaw Memorial and the new gymnasium. The handbook mentioned above describes the equipment in considerable detail. The steam was used for generating the University's electricity and it was also piped to all the campus buildings to supply heat. When we consider that electricity was a new phenomenon for lighting, it is not surprising that the author brags that the "Plant has been equipped with the most modern machinery for producing heat and light and is well worth visiting."

With two major buildings on the eastern and southern sides of it, Brokaw Hall was tucked into the corner of a large "L." Although overpowered by the sheer size of its neighbors, it never lost its separate identity.

Publisher: Not Indicated * Manufacturer: Not Indicated * Type: Photograph, Divided Back * Postmark: Not Used * Value Index: C

Bird's eye view postcards were popular in the era when postcards were in their greatest use, as views from an airplane are today. This photograph was probably taken from the roof of Patton Hall, which was completed in 1906. The picture had to be taken in that year. The author's collection has a postcard of the same scene postmarked 1907. Shown from left to right, you see the two sections of Stafford Little Hall, and the round roof of Halstead Observatory is visible over the roof of Blair Hall. To the right of Blair Tower, Witherspoon Hall dominates the center, and Edwards Hall is at the right.

Edwards Hall was named after Jonathan Edwards, famed theologian, third president of the College of New Jersey, father-in-law of Aaron Burr, Sr., second president, and grandfather of the distinguished (or notorious) Aaron Burr, Jr., Vice-President of the United States. The dormitory was built at the request of President McCosh to provide inexpensive accommodations for students of modest means and reduce the number of students who lived in the village. Also, an important reason behind its construction was to balance the luxury of the new Witherspoon Hall. President McCosh was concerned that the school was being viewed as a rich man's college. In a simplistic vein, the dormitory was considered to be occupied by poorer, and therefore brainier, students. It was dubbed "Poler's Paradise," "Poler" being a term which was replaced by "Grind," or perhaps "Greasy Grind." Interestingly enough, early in this century, a returning alumnus commented, "Believe it or not, Witherspoon and Edwards were comparatively new and much admired buildings."

Patton Hall, Princeton University.

Publisher: W. C. Sinclair, Princeton, NJ * Manufacturer: The Albertype Co., Brooklyn, NY * Type: Black and White, Divided Back * Postmark: Not Used * Value Index: E

Princeton College. Princeton N. J.

No. 125 Published for The American News Company, New York, Leipzig-Berlin

Publisher: American News Co., NY, Leipzig, Berlin, Card No. 125 * Manufacturer: American News Co., NY, Leipzig, Berlin * Type: Black and White, Red Imprint, Undivided Back * Postmark: Not Used * Value Index: B

Before World War II, Patton Hall was the last dormitory to the south of the main campus. Compensating for its remoteness from classroom buildings and the library, however, were the nearby gymnasium, tennis courts, and recreational athletic fields. This photograph shows the dormitory beyond the tennis courts which were behind the gymnasium and power-house.

In the original interior layout of Nassau Hall, the hallways ran the length of the building. The design was probably an important factor in spreading the flames during the two great fires, but it also facilitated the student insurrections and riots which were so common for a century or more. Later dormitory buildings were made up of separate contiguous sections, or "Entries." Patton Hall was financed by alumni of ten classes—one for each of the ten entries. The dormitory was named for President Francis Landey Patton, who was in office when the College of New Jersey became Princeton University. He was highly respected and loved as a teacher and speaker, but he was not a successful administrator. The trustees convinced him to resign, and Woodrow Wilson, with Patton's blessing, was immediately selected to fill the post. Patton continued as a teacher, however, and almost immediately was appointed to fill the new position of President of Princeton Theological Seminary. It is interesting to note that Patton Hall is the only building on the campus named for a president of the college during his lifetime.

This view is what visitors saw when they walked from the railroad station up the steps and through the arch of Blair Tower. Again, Witherspoon Hall dominates the scene and dwarfs West College on the left. The walkway in front of Witherspoon Hall begins at Blair Tower and forms the rear boundary of Cannon Green in front of Clio and Whig Halls, but it previously terminated at Marquand Chapel. In this photograph, the latter is barely visible next to the corner of West College.

Although the person who sent this postcard obeyed the law by not writing the message on the address side, he (or she) must have had a change of mind. It was undoubtedly mailed in an envelope, because there is nothing written on the back.

The campus must have been a gloomy place after that last football game of the season. In that era, Princeton-Yale was THE game—Harvard was not on the Princeton schedule from 1897 through 1910. Although the 1904 record was eight wins and two losses, the season was considered to be sub-par. After all, the team had had an undefeated eleven-game season the year before, and for the previous three years, Princeton had won twenty-eight games, tied one, and lost only two. The three-year .903 record was only slightly eroded by the 1904 season; Princetonians of today would be glad to have similar bragging rights.

HISTORIC CANNON ON PRINCETON UNIVERSITY
CAMPUS, PRINCETON, N. J.

Pub. by Edw G. van Marter

Publisher: Edward G. van Marter, Princeton, NJ * Manufacturer: Not Indicated * Type: Colored, Divided Back * Postmark: Not Used * Value Index: E

Campus Princeton Univ. showing Reunion College offices and Dean's Residence.

Publisher: Van Marter, Princeton, NJ * Manufacturer: N. N., Distributed by E. W. Fausnaugh, Printed in Germany * Type: Colored, Divided Back * Postmark: Not Used * Value Index: E

This view of the Big Cannon looks east, past the corner of Pyne Library, towards Marquand Chapel dimly seen in the background. A well-travelled relic of the Battle of Princeton in 1777, sixty-three years passed before it was partially buried, muzzle down, in its place of honor behind Nassau Hall. Because its carriage was broken, it was abandoned in the village by both the British and Americans. When the War of 1812 broke out, it was sent to defend New Brunswick, where it lay for fifteen years on the town common. In 1827, Princeton townspeople rescued it, but their wagon broke down in Queenston (near the present intersection of Nassau and Harrison Streets). It was not until 1838 that a group of students retrieved it and brought it to the front campus, to the great dismay of the college authorities. Obviously, dismay did not lead to action; the cannon was finally sunk in its present place in 1840.

About the time this photograph was taken, one author described the cannon as "The great totem of the place and about it the life of a Princeton undergraduate begins and ends." This was where there used to be an annual battle between the Freshmen and Sophomores called the "Rush." In a more sedate role, it was the scene for Seniors to gather for their last graduation ceremonies. It is still the scene of celebratory bonfires to mark a football victory or other event of importance to the students.

The caption on the postcard is misleading. West College (1836) dominates the foreground, Reunion Hall (1870) is partially obscured by trees, and Stanhope Hall (1803) and the Dean's Residence are in the background.

The late President of the United States, John Fitzgerald Kennedy, matriculated at Princeton University in 1935 as a member of the Class of 1939. Unfortunately, he was ill and was forced to withdraw in less than two months. While on campus, he roomed in Reunion Hall. Although the building was razed as a fire hazard in 1965, his presence on the campus is memorialized in the Class of 1939 Dormitory. In retrospect, it is interesting to note that as an applicant he wrote, "To be a Princeton Man is indeed an enviable distinction."

Reunion Hall was named to commemorate the reunion of the Old and New Schools of the Presbyterian Church. Major theological disagreements had split the denomination for many years, and the building of this dormitory celebrated the coming together of the warring groups. Both segments supplied funds for its construction, and officers of the General Assembly of the Presbyterian Church presided at the laying of the cornerstone. To provide room for the new building the home of Joseph Henry, a famous physicist, made the first of its several moves about the campus.

West College was built in 1836 as the twin second dormitory to the college's first dormitory, East College (1833). When it was completed, the layout of buildings on the campus was completely symmetrical. Nassau Hall fronted on the town and dominated the northern boundary of what is now Cannon Green. On the western boundary, Stanhope Hall and West College looked across the green at their identical counterparts, Philosophical Hall and East College. From the south, the twin Greek temples of Whig and Clio Halls faced the back of Nassau Hall. The first crack in the symmetry came in 1873, when Philosophical Hall was levelled to make way for the Chancellor Green Library. The

West College
Princeton University

Publisher: The Princeton University Store, Princeton, NJ * Manufacturer: The Albertype Co., Brooklyn, NY * Type: Sepia, Divided Back * Postmark: Not Used * Value Index: C

final break came when East College was replaced by the Pyne Library. The loss of the old dormitory was mourned by many alumni as "The Crime of Ninety-Six."

The Princeton University Store, first familiarly known as "The Uni-Vee Store," now commonly called "The U-Store," was housed in West College from its inception in 1896 until it moved to its own quarters at its present location in 1958. A cooperative society, it is patronized by both town and gown. The dormitory was converted to offices in the 1960s.

This photograph of Cannon Green looks south between Whig and Clio Halls. Note that there is no walkway or road between the Halls, yet an early automobile is heading toward the photographer. When examined under a glass, the vehicle appears to be an old-fashioned touring car, a multipassenger "Rag-Top" model which was so popular at that time.

Approximately where the automobile is shown in the photograph was the famous Cloaca Maxima. For well over a century, wooden privies dotted the campus. The students, however, considered them fair game, and a favorite diversion was to set fire to the little buildings. To solve this ever-present problem, the college built a fireproof facility below ground-level, and dignified it with this tongue-twisting Latin

Publisher: Not Indicated * Manufacturer: Not Indicated * Type: Photograph, Divided Back * Postmark: Not Used * Value Index: C

name. Although the Cloaco Maxima was not an unqualified success, the problem was finally resolved at the turn of the 20th century by the introduction of sanitary plumbing.

Hazing and interclass rivalries were serious business and contributed a considerable amount of work for the college infirmary. Many of the rivalries were contested on Cannon Green. One historical reference records that "In the fall of 1904 two freshman were knocked cold in the annual rush with the sophomores. By their thoughtless actions they jinxed the year athletically." A dismal litany of tragic athletic losses followed.

Simply known today as Dod Hall, the full name of this dormitory was Albert B. Dod Hall. The suites consisted of a study and one or two bedrooms, and the building housed over 100 students. Architecturally, it was described as "Italianate" or "Romanesque," but it was not particularly admired. One critic said that its features "robbed the structure of architectural charm." A kinder comment was that it "had its harsh exterior softened by ivy." The students, however, took a practical approach. The dormitory was very popular, because it was roomy and well lighted.

ALBERT B. DOD HALL, PRINCETON, N. J.

Publisher: Christie Whiteman, Princeton, NJ * Manufacturer: Probably Curt Teich, Chicago, IL * Type: Colored, White Border, Divided Back * Postmark: Not Used * Value Index: E

The building was given by Mrs. David Brown in memory of her brother, Professor Albert Baldwin Dod, Class of 1822. A brilliant student and teacher, Dr. Dod matriculated at age 15, graduated at 17, and was appointed Professor of Mathematics at age 25. Along the way, he also received a degree from Princeton Theological Seminary. Considered to be the greatest teacher of mathematics of his time, he was also extremely versatile. In addition, he taught architecture, political economy, and was an inspirational preacher. His untimely death at age 40 was termed "a tremendous blow to the college," and Princeton lost one of its truly great teachers.

This postcard was sent by a campus visitor to a lady in Topsham, Maine. The message says, "I do not think this is a very artistic looking building, do you? Doesn't quite come up to Walker Art Gallery at old Bowdoin, does it?" The critic was perceptive, but she probably did not know why. The Museum of Historic Art was dedicated in 1887; it was never completed. The original plans called for an added wing at each end and an extension to the rear to provide space for classrooms and a lecture hall. After 34 years, when academic pressures mandated expansion, McCormick Hall was added to the west end in 1921. In 1964, 43 years later, the old museum was demolished and replaced by the present Art Museum

Art Museum, Princeton University, Princeton, N. J.

Publisher: Illustrated Postal Card Co., NY, Card No. 99.1 * Manufacturer: Illustrated Postal Card Co., NY, Germany * Type: Colored, Undivided Back * Postmark: Not Used * Value Index E

building. It has been said that had it been completed according to plan, it would have been a fine example of Romanesque architecture.

Publisher: Not Indicated, Card No. 63842 * Manufacturer: Not Indicated * Type: Colored, Divided Back * Postmark: Not Used * Value Index: E

Publisher: A. C. Bosselman & Co., NY, Card No. 891 * Manufacturer: Made in Germany * Type: Colored, Undivided Back * Postmark: Not Used * Value Index: E

This particular postcard is a good example of one which was mailed in a covering envelope. In this instance, the writer may have been protecting her message from prying eyes. On the back she has simply scrawled, "Sorry you are so mean to Ma. Try to come down to the fair. Harold from Cora."

Just as Whig and Clio Halls have the same physical identity, it is almost impossible to discuss them separately in a brief survey. The American Whig Society and the Cliosophic Society were secret literary and debating societies with roots going back to 1769. They were always intensely competitive, and until the late 19th century were the centers for the daily life of undergraduates. Failure to receive an invitation to join either Whig or Clio led to a difficult existence on campus. (Later a student who failed to be selected by an eating club became somewhat of a campus failure.) Debate was the center of activity, and hundreds of men honed their speaking skills in the halls.

The early growth of the societies led to the construction of twin Greek temples in 1838. With the expansion of enrollment, curriculum, and social opportunities in the late 1800s, interest among the students began to decline. As one step towards restoring their pre-eminence on campus, the wood and stucco halls were replicated in marble. The cornerstones were laid in 1890 by President Patton and Ex-President McCosh.

The new buildings could not halt the decline. In 1929 the societies merged to form American Whig-Cliosophic Society with headquarters in Whig Hall. A fire in 1969 gutted the building, but only the eastern exterior wall had to be replaced. Immediate restoration restored the home of a vital campus organization.

From the earliest days, the organization and functioning of the two literary societies were secrets as closely held as those for any fraternal organization in the outside world. For example, the massive front doors had combination locks; only members knew the combinations. The training for debate which took place within the two Greek temples served well in preparing teams for the Annual Triangular Debate with Yale and Harvard. Interest in this event rivaled that of a football championship. If Princeton and Yale were debating at Princeton, Alexander Hall would be packed. At the same time another team would be debating Harvard at Cambridge. A Princeton victory at home meant that the audience would remain in Alexander Hall until the telegram with the Harvard results was received. If Princeton won both debates, there was a celebration which was probably topped off by a spontaneous midnight parade (spelled "P-rade" in Princeton).

When Greek letter fraternities appeared on the campus in the mid-19th century, the authorities moved to suppress them. One of the reasons given was that they would erode the status of Whig and Clio. After several decades of controversy, they were eliminated. Oddly enough, not many seemed to perceive that the growth of the eating clubs posed a similar threat to the literary societies.

The postcards always pictured "The Halls" on a calm, serene (and usually deserted) campus. Until the 1920s, however, the front steps of the buildings were the scene of a spectacular and messy bit of mass hazing. The freshman class picture was taken on the steps, but the sophomores thoughtfully bombarded them with flour bombs and rotten fruit, followed by a thorough hosing down.

As one writer commented, "With Brown Hall, experimentation ceased; henceforth, Collegiate Gothic was to be the architectural style for the Princeton Campus." To give the Hall its full name, David Brown Hall (1892) was modeled after a Florentine palace, and its 50 suites housed 140 students. Given by the same donor as Albert B. Dod Hall, it shares similar criticisms and compliments. One commentator said that Dod Hall was "a thing of beauty . . . when compared to David Brown Hall," but Brown Hall was also a popular dormitory among the students. Its rooms were "sunnier and more comfortably arranged," and many of them enjoyed beautiful vistas across Lake Carnegie and the countryside. On the eastern side, the students looked down on Prospect Gardens, which were so lovingly developed by Mrs. Woodrow Wilson.

PRINCETON UNIVERSITY. David Brown Hall.

Publisher: Raphael Tuck & Sons, London, England, "Princeton University," Card No. 5663 * Manufacturer: Raphael Tuck & Sons, London, England, Printed in Holland * Type: Colored, Undivided Back * Postmark: Not Used * Value Index: E

A returning alumnus reminisced about an exciting event of his undergraduate days. At commencement time, a band from Annapolis was giving a concert when a fire broke out in David Brown Hall. Although it apparently was not serious, his recollection was that "The City Fire Department responded promptly a few days later."

Cuyler Hall was named for an alumnus who had the unusual name of Cornelius Cuyler Cuyler. A banker who served as a university trustee for over a decade before his death in 1909, he was a member of the influential Class of 1879. At the dedication of the dormitory in 1912, his classmate, Woodrow Wilson, the new Governor of New Jersey, gave the dedication address.

The plans for developing the area immediately to the east of Brown, Cuyler, and Patton Halls were disrupted by the intervention of World War I and the moving of the Pennsylvania Railroad Station from the foot of the Blair Hall steps to its present location. No dormitories were constructed in this area for the next 17 years. After the Great War, the university was busy building

CUYLER HALL, PRINCETON UNIVERSITY.

Publisher: Princeton University Store, Princeton, NJ * Manufacturer: The Albertype Co., Brooklyn, NY * Type: Sepia, Divided Back * Postmark: Not Used * Value Index: D

on the old railroad right-of-way along University Place. Between 1922 and 1927, Pyne, Foulke, Henry, Laughlin and Lockhart dormitories were completed.

Prospect President's Residence, Princeton University, Princeton N. J.

Published by Edw. J. van Marter. Printed in Germany

Publisher: Edw. J. Van Marter, Princeton, NJ * Manufacturer: Printed in Germany * Type: Colored, Undivided Back * Postmark: Not Used * Value Index: E

In 1878, when Prospect was given to the college for use as the president's home, the acquisition almost tripled the size of the campus. The donors, the Stuart brothers, were the same staunch Presbyterians who gave Stuart Hall to the Princeton Theological Seminary. This view from the gardens was published not long after the new president, Woodrow Wilson, took up residence. His wife, Ellen, loved flowers, and one of her major interests was the development of Prospect Gardens, which are still one of the show pieces of Princeton. When students and football crowds thoughtlessly trampled her gardens, an angry Dr. Wilson had the property enclosed with a wrought iron fence.

In 1906, President Theodore Roosevelt and his entourage had lunch at Prospect with the Wilsons before attending the Army and Navy football game, which was held on University Field. Ellen Wilson's young sister, Madge, related that the boisterous President teased her all during the meal with an "appalling roar" and "slam-banging" on the table. Her date, who was waiting outside, asked about the uproar and she concluded her explanation with the comment that "If that's the way Presidents behave, I hope to the Lord I never meet another." Only six years later her brother-in-law was elected to the Presidency of the United States.

In this era, meetings of trustees were held at Prospect. Before the annual commencement, the recipients of various honors at graduation were approved so that they could be announced at exercises. Of course, the list was a closely held secret. This was a major problem for the Daily Princetonian, which published a special edition containing a transcript of the proceedings. It was sold to the audience as the attendees left the Hall. Moses Taylor Pyne, who was very popular among the students, sympathized with this dilemma. After the trustees approved the awards, he would casually go to a window, and a copy of the precious list would accidentally drift down to the waiting hands of a student editor.

In 1968, after 90 years of service as the President's residence, the off-campus Walter Lowrie House became the new home for presidents. Prospect was converted and remodeled into a dining and social center for the university staff. Coincidentally, both Prospect and Walter Lowrie House were built about the same time, and both were designed by John Notman, a famous Philadelphia architect.

Murray-Dodge Hall is actually two separate buildings connected by a cloister. Each is a memorial to an alumnus who died shortly after graduation. Hamilton Murray, "A young man honored for his seriousness and piety," was lost at sea a year after his graduation in 1872. In his will, he left $20,000 to the college for the building. The funds for the companion building, built in 1900, were given by the Dodge family in memory of W. Earl Dodge, Jr., Class of 1879, who lived for only five years after graduation. He, too, had been active in campus and community religious activities, so it was appropriate that Murray-Dodge Hall became the headquarters for the religious and social work of the college community. The principal tenant was the Philadelphian Society, the oldest collegiate religious organization in the country. Its activities were not limited to the campus. It sponsored a local club for men and boys of the village, it operated a summer camp for "city boys," and it reached all the way to Peking, China, to found and staff the Peking Y.M.C.A. With the secularization of the college activities, the role of Murray-Dodge Hall has been modified. The small "auditorium for public worship" in Murray is now devoted to theatrical productions, but campus religious and social service organizations still have offices in Dodge.

Publisher: Princeton University Store, Princeton, NJ, Card No. AA4775 * Manufacturer: American News Co., NY, Leipzig, Dresden, Berlin, "Steeldrucktone," Made in Germany * Type: Sepia, Divided Back * Postmark: Not Used * Value Index: E

The bigger-than-life statue called the "Christian Student" memorialized W. Earl Dodge, Jr., who was also remembered through the gift of Dodge Hall. He was an honor student, and athlete. His greatest honor was spelled out on the base of the statue. On the front, it states that the statue is "To mark the birthplace of the world-wide union of Christian students in work for Christ," and the side panel says, "1876— Nearby—some words by William E. Dodge, Junior, led a little group of students to form the Intercollegiate Young Men's Christian Association from which the student volunteer movement and world's Christian Student Federation has grown."

Sometimes called the "Christian Athlete" in error, it was the work of sculptor, Daniel

"Statue" at Princeton University, Princeton, N. J.

Publisher: Christie Whiteman, Princeton, NJ * Manufacturer: Probably Curt Teich Co., Chicago, IL, or Brooklyn Post Card Co., Inc., New York, NY * Type: Colored, Divided Back * Postmark: June 1, 1922 * Value Index: C

Chester French, who is best known for the seated Lincoln in the Lincoln Memorial, Washington, D.C. During the 1920s, it became the target for student pranks and was twice torn from its pedestal. It was loaned to the Daniel Chester French Museum in Stockbridge, Massachusetts. Through the efforts of Hugh de N. Wynne, Class of 1939, the statue was returned to the campus and is installed in the lobby of Jadwin Gymnasium.

This postcard is doubly interesting; it shows the Joseph Henry House. For some unfathomable reason, the publishers never marketed a postcard for this famous home. As shown on this postcard, the building was always ancillary to the main subject and was never identified. The house was built in 1837 for Joseph Henry, world-famous physicist, and arguably the true inventor of the magnetic telegraph. Long before the commercial telegraph, Henry communicated to his house from his office over a wire which stretched between the two buildings. He left Princeton to become the first Secretary of the Smithsonian Institution. The trustees tried to lure him back, but he refused even when offered the presidency of the college.

McCosh Hall, Princeton University, Princeton, N. J.

Publisher: Christie Whiteman, Princeton, NJ * Manufacturer: Not Indicated * Type: Colored, Divided Back * Postmark: Not Used * Value Index: D

The "campaign" to raise funds for the construction of McCosh Hall provides a fascinating embellishment to the history of Princeton University. In 1877, a handful of students in the south entry of the East College dormitory formed the South East Club. After graduation, the club was perpetuated by meeting for dinner twice a year, once in Princeton and once in the New York area. Five members became trustees, and all were generous donors. After one dinner, when the conversation turned to university affairs, it was agreed that the need for additional classroom space was critical. Cleveland H. Dodge turned to his classmate, Moses Taylor Pyne, and casually offered to "Go you halves on a new building." The quarter million dollars was quickly raised, and McCosh Hall with its four large lecture halls, 14 classrooms, and 20 small rooms for use by Woodrow Wilson's new preceptors, was dedicated in 1906.

When it was built, McCosh Hall was the largest building on the campus. The rear of the wing, to the right on the postcard, stretches for 400 feet along McCosh walk, and the wing behind the sundial in the grassy circle extends for 100 feet along Washington Road. The somewhat unfinished wall below the tower shows that construction was to continue. The planned court around the sundial was not completed for almost another quarter of a century when the new Dickinson Hall and University Chapel were completed.

The imposing Mather Sun Dial was given by Sir William Mather as a symbol of academic and national ties between Oxford University and Princeton University. It is a replica of a 1551 sundial at Oxford. For many years, only seniors were privileged to sit on the steps. Offenders were undoubtedly subjected to swift punishment.

The plot of land shown on the postcard was a pawn in the controversy over the location of the graduate school. Shortly after acquiring the property, it was designated for the planned school, but Woodrow Wilson built McCosh Hall there instead. Dean Alexander West, the other protagonist in the graduate school battle, gradually shifted his emphasis to locating the buildings on the golf course grounds, where they stand today.

MARQUAND CHAPEL.   PRINCETON UNIVERSITY.

Publisher: Princeton University Store, Princeton, NJ * Manufacturer: The Albertype Co., Brooklyn, NY * Type: Sepia, Divided Back * Postmark: Not Used * Value Index: D

Publisher: Van Marter, Princeton, NJ, Card No. 2489/32 * Manufacturer: Printed in Germany * Type: Colored, Divided Back * Postmark: Not Used * Value Index: C

The postcard clearly shows the Christian Student and Joseph Henry House as well as the stone Marquand Chapel. The road in front of the chapel came from Nassau Street to the left of the picture and terminated at Prospect to the right. The road in the foreground still crosses the campus toward Blair Hall and passes in front of Whig, Clio, and Witherspoon Halls.

Until 1847, chapel services (always compulsory for the students) were held in the prayer hall of Nassau Hall. When the first separate chapel was being built, its construction was almost cancelled when conservative trustees discovered that it was cruciform. However, economics overcame the fear of "Popery." There were also concerns over the "worldly" organ; the complainers apparently were not aware that the original prayer hall in Nassau Hall included such a musical instrument. Growth of the student body demanded a more spacious facility; Marquand Chapel was dedicated by President McCosh at the baccalaureate service in 1882.

During the house-parties weekend in 1920, the eating clubs were in their social whirl on Prospect Avenue and the freshmen were holding a dance in the gymnasium. Fire broke out in Dickinson Hall, which then stood to the left of the Joseph Henry House. The local volunteer firemen, students in evening clothes, and firemen from Trenton fought the conflagration, but could do little but to protect the smaller buildings nearby. Unaccountably, the fire leap-frogged over the Joseph Henry House and destroyed Marquand Chapel, but the house was only singed.

A footnote on the Joseph Henry House is the fact that it is probably the most travelled one in Princeton. The community has many buildings which have been moved, but this one is currently in its fourth location on the campus. Originally it stood next to Stanhope Hall at the western end of Nassau Hall. When Reunion Hall was built, it was moved to the location shown on the postcard. The next move was to the southwest corner of Nassau Street and Washington Road to clear room for the present University Chapel, and the final(?) move was made to permit construction of the Firestone Library at that corner.

The architecture of the chapel sanctuary foreshadowed that of Alexander Hall by a decade. Under natural light, there must have been a kaleidoscope of colors, because all of the windows were of stained glass, several of them by Tiffany. It is unfortunate that the postcard shows only the smaller windows in the apse; the major windows were on the other three walls. When you note the wooden pews, wainscoting, ceilings, and doors, and visualize the wood framing and lath behind the plastered walls, it is not surprising that an apparently invulnerable stone building could be destroyed by fire in one night.

On the wall at the left center of the picture is a bronze relief portrait of Dr. McCosh by Augustus St. Gaudens. Only his head survived the fire. When the new chapel was built in the late 1920s, it was found that the sculptor's model had been preserved for almost one-half century, and a duplicate bronze was cast. It looks down on the pews in the Marquand Transept of the present University Chapel. Compulsory attendance at chapel was never popular among the students, and over the years the requirements were made less stringent. At first, services were twice a day, but by the 1890s chapel attendance was required once each day, and twice on Sunday. By World War I students had to attend weekday services at least twice each week and at least one-half of the Sunday services in each quarter. After World War II, regulations for required chapel attendance gradually disappeared.

Publisher: Not Indicated * Manufacturer: Not Indicated * Type: Photograph,
Divided Back * Postmark: Not Used * Value Index: B

Publisher: Raphael Tuck & Sons, London, England, Card Series 2069, "Prin. Univ." * Manufacturer: Raphael Tuck & Sons,
London, England * Type: colored, Undivided Back * Postmark: Not Used * Value Index: E

This famous photograph shows James McCosh, President of the College of New Jersey from 1868 to 1888, taking a stroll on the walk named for him. The postcard must have been printed from an old glass plate negative, because he died in 1894, before the advent of the postcard era. The land on the other side of the picket fence at the right was not then owned by the college; it later became the site of McCosh Hall.

There is a mystery concerned with this particular photograph. In other publications it includes a man and women watching the photographer from the background. Because they are standing about 75 feet behind and to the left of President McCosh, they do not seriously intrude on the picture. The postcard must have been made from a skillfully touched up negative.

In the 150 years before the college was renamed Princeton University, the two giants among the presidents were John Witherspoon and James McCosh. By uncanny coincidence, their lives paralleled each other.

For example,
—they were born in Scotland
—they were educated at the University of Edinburgh
—they were world-renowned ministers in the Church of Scotland
—they were installed as presidents of the College exactly 100 years apart; 1768 and 1868
—they had to rebuild the college after the devastation of war
—they died one century and one day apart; November 15, 1794 and November 16, 1894

In his twenty years as president, Dr. McCosh made far-reaching changes in the college. He added many buildings to the campus and also added to and strengthened the curriculum and faculty. Among his crowning achievements were the building up of an outstanding library, the creation of a school of science and engineering, and the establishment of a graduate school. At the same time, his love of horticulture led to the transformation of a rather scruffy campus to a beautiful park-like academic setting. He laid the foundations for the emergence of the new Princeton University in 1896.

It can be assumed that the formal name of Pyne Library never caught on with the college community. The early postcards simply identified it as the "New Library," and the school maps joined it with the earlier Chancellor Green Library as the "University Library." There is no question, however, that the two buildings were keys to the reshaping of the central campus both in plan and style. Until Chancellor Green Library was built in 1873, the college buildings were symmetrically balanced. Stanhope Hall was matched by the identical Philosophical Hall at the east end of Nassau Hall, East College and West College dormitories faced each other across the Cannon Green, and of course, the twin Whig and Clio Halls stood on the southern border. The first library replaced Philosophical Hall with a more ornate architectural style next to Nassau Hall. The new, and much larger, addition of Pyne Library introduced the Collegiate Gothic style to the main campus and spelled the doom of East College.

For the celebration of the college's sesquicentennial in 1896, Moses Taylor Pyne, as Chairman of the Trustee's Committee on Grounds and Buildings, had plans drawn for a library addition and a handful of other major buildings. This device for enticing commemorative gifts was very successful; Pyne himself induced his mother to give the Pyne Library. When East College was razed, the graduating students had a glorious bonfire of the doors and other wood from the building, but it ignited a different kind of fire among the alumni. Six decades of students had made their home in East College, and they did not hesitate to express their feelings over the loss of this landmark. They were also critical of the new type of architecture and the final break in the symmetry of the main campus. This brouhaha was promptly dubbed "The Crime of Ninety-Six." It is interesting to speculate whether the project would have gone forward if the donor trustee himself had not been an East College resident and a leader of the powerful and respected South East Club.

Entrance to Library Courtyard, Princeton University, Princeton, N. J.

Publisher: Illustrated Postal Card Co., NY, Card No. 99.-6 * Manufacturer: Illustrated Postal Card Co., NY, Germany * Type: Colored, Undivided Back * Postmark: Not Used * Value Index: E

-YARD, PRINCE
PRINCETON, N. J.

Publisher: Edward G. van Marter, Princeton, NJ * Manufacturer: Printed in Germany * Type: Colored, Divided Back * Postmark: Not Used * Value Index: C

How many students have John Witherspoon and James McCosh surveyed from their niches over this lovely entrance from Cannon Green? For the students, this was not their principal access to the library. The main entrances were in the link connecting the old and new buildings. The card catalogue and delivery desk were located there and all of the books were moved to stacks in the new building. Open stacks were unknown; they were a mid-20th century innovation. The old Chancellor Green Library was converted into a reading and reference room.

The new building was the fifth home for the college library. When Aaron Burr, Sr., moved the school into the newly built Nassau Hall, the collection of 474 volumes was housed in a room directly over the center entrance. After the fire of 1802, a new building was named the Library (now Stanhope Hall), although it also had classrooms and was the home of Whig and Clio Societies. The second great fire in Nassau Hall indirectly led to the return of the library to that building. The restoration of "Old North" provided adequate space in the former prayer hall. When Dr. McCosh assumed the presidency, he was horrified to find a paltry collection of books accessible to the students for only one hour per week! Within five years, he had acquired Chancellor Green Library, the first building on the campus devoted exclusively to that function. He also hired the college's first full-time librarian. The new building was quickly outgrown, and Pyne Library answered the desperate need for additional space. It increased the library capacity by a factor of ten.

This is a view of the courtyard after walking through the entrance shown on the previous postcard. Note that the interior wall has been provided with four ornate niches for additional statuary. Through the arch, there is a rather indistinct view of the path as it extends toward William Street. The architect used good judgment in providing the archways, because it preserved the existing straight pathway to Washington Road and access to the rapidly developing Prospect Street.

William Street—named for William Clow, an early steward of the college—has an interesting history. Maps of the mid-1800s show that it was a short stub of a street running from Washington Road to within a few feet of Pyne Hall's east wall. There was no street running east from Washington Road. The campus portion became a pathway, but the university did not officially obtain title to the land until the 1930s.

Over the years, the growth of the library was anything but consistent. Despite the ravages of occupation during the Revolution, the original 474 volumes grew to 3,000 in 1802, the year of the first devastating fire. Only 100 volumes survived the fire and alumni and friends were galvanized into action to restore the books. There were 7,000 volumes in 1812, but during the next 40 years, the college's period of stagnation, the total grew only to 9,000! When Dr. McCosh arrived on the scene in 1868, there were 14,000 volumes, and under his leadership, the library became a vitally important cog in the academic machine. When Chancellor Green Library opened in 1873, 25,000 volumes were in a facility which could accommodate 70,000 volumes. The euphoric period was short-lived. In a decade, the library was at capacity with thousands of books stored in the damp cellar. When the Pyne addition opened the pair of buildings had a capacity of 1,250,000 volumes, and one optimistic writer estimated that it would take two hundred years to fill. The reality was that the problem of over-crowding returned in the 1920s, but the Depression and World War II prevented any corrective action until the late 1940s, when the Firestone Library opened.

Publisher: Not Indicated * Manufacturer: Not Indicated * Type: Photograph, Divided Back * Postmark: Not Used * Value Index: B

Publisher: Edward G. Van Marter, Princeton, NJ, Card No. 868/8 * Manufacturer: N. N., Distributed by E. W. Fausnaugh, Printed in Germany * Type: Colored, Divided Back * Postmark: Not Used * Value Index: C

The octagon-shaped Chancellor Green Library with its smaller octagonal appendages on the east and west sides was not a subject for early postcards, probably because the Pyne Library addition was new, much larger, and thoroughly modern. Judged to be one of the major library buildings in the country, the purveyors of postcards undoubtedly considered Pyne Library to be a "hot seller" and the old building to be "old hat."

The photograph shows the interior of Chancellor Green after it had become the reading and reference room for the library complex. Through the door at the left center can be seen the delivery desk in the link which connected the new building to the old building. The trestle tables in the foreground appear to be the repositories for the periodicals and daily newspapers. Within view of the camera, only one chair and a single bench are visible in this reading room. Where did the students sit?

When the trustees approved the design of Chancellor Green Library they liked it so much that they insisted on placing it in a prominent spot on the front campus. To do this, Philosophical Hall, where Joseph Henry had done his pioneer work on the telegraph, was razed. The destruction of the twin to Stanhope Hall was also the first major breach in the symmetry of the campus layout.

When it was the main library, three additional stacks were placed in the balcony between each of the stacks in the photograph. More stacks were located on the main floor. There was little or no room for students to linger and study. Reading was by natural light; no artificial illumination was provided. As one author put it, "Its stained glass and inadequate lighting was a menace to good eyesight." After McCosh's revolutionary edict to keep the library open until dusk for six days each week, the librarian informed the trustees that if the library were illuminated, he thought that the students would be willing to come into the library during the evening. At the time this picture was taken, small clusters of electric lights are visible beneath the balcony railings.

This rather forbidding brick and stone building is located on the southeast corner of Nassau Street and Washington Road. The structure behind it, the Civil Engineering Laboratory (1904) was another subject which the publishers did not deem worthy for immortalizing on a postcard. The view along Nassau Street is virtually the same today, except that Washington Road seems to have been narrower when this picture was taken. Of course, in the interim the streets have been paved and decorated with parking meters.

This postcard of the Chemical Laboratory (1891) illustrates several milestones in the physical expansion and growth of the university. The plot of land, purchased by John Cleve Green's brother Caleb in 1882, was the first property on Nassau Street acquired by the college to the east of Washington Road. The 1974 purchase of the Mershon house, the first one next to the laboratory, completed university ownership of the block bounded by Washington Road and Charlton, William and Nassau Streets. The laboratory itself was the final building given by the John Cleve Green Estate.

The laboratory was built to relieve the over-taxed John C. Green School of Science located directly across Washington Road. It was a mixture of laboratories, offices, and lecture rooms, but the top floor was devoted to student laboratories. As one author put it, "for forty years undergraduates unflinchingly endured its pervasive smells." After it was succeeded by more modern facilities, it became the School of Engineering Annex. It now houses the Department of Anthropology and other offices. In 1977, it was renamed Aaron Burr Hall after the second President of the College of New Jersey (1748-1757) who led the college when it moved to Princeton.

Publisher: Raphael Tuck & Sons, London, England, Card Series No. 2069, "Prin. Univ." * Manufacturer: Raphael Tuck & Sons, London, England * Type: Colored, Undivided Back * Postmark: Not Used * Value Index: D

Publisher: Raphael Tuck & Sons, London, England, Card Series No. 2069, "Prin. Univ." * Manufacturer: Raphael Tuck & Sons, London, England * Type: Colored, Undivided Back * Postmark: Not Used * Value Index: E

A hallmark of the postcards published by Raphael Tuck & Sons was that they included people, a rare feature on most view cards. Examination of the scenes leads one to suspect that the human figures were sometimes superimposed on the photograph to add interest. On the left, partially obscured by the bush, is the Class of 1877 Laboratory. There are no known postcards with this modest building as the subject, although it stood on the front campus for 60 years. In all probability, the publishers did not think such postcards would sell.

When McCosh came on the scene, one of his top priorities was the addition of new classrooms. Those in use when he arrived were gloomy and overcrowded, and the better ones shared space with laboratories or museum exhibits. One critic described the rooms as "mostly illconditioned cellars and attics." When the weather was cold, the benches often disappeared into the stove to provide a bit of warmth. Dickinson Hall was the first Princeton building devoted to classroom and lecture space. A special feature was the top floor of the building. It was planned as an examination hall, an area dreaded by generations of students. This new addition to the campus gave McCosh the physical facility for his planned expansion of academic offerings.

As with the Chancellor Green Library, McCosh was very proud of "the stately structure of Dickenson Hall." In its day it was much admired, but when the enthusiasm for Victorian Architecture waned, one critic dismissed it by saying that "It contains little of interest." Another merely described it as "grim." After the 1920 holocaust, when both Dickinson Hall and Marquand Chapel were destroyed by fire, there was little mourning over the loss of the classroom building.

The John C. Green School of Science (1873) was located on the campus at approximately the same spot as today's Firestone Library. From the entrance steps at the foot of the clock tower, visitors had an excellent view of sleepy Nassau Street and the campus along the front of Dickinson Hall toward Chancellor Green Library. As with Dickenson Hall, the School of Science was initially considered beautiful, but later critics used descriptive terms such as "architectural monstrosity."

The science faculty was, for the first time, provided with adequate lecture halls, laboratories, a photography room, museum space, and offices. However, within a very few years, the growth of the scientific and engineering fields brought back the old problems of overcrowding. One physicist reminisced that he was assigned a space in "a kind of dark basement, ventilated by a hole in the wall" to establish a research laboratory. For company, he had "an impressive colony of hoptoads which enjoyed the use of a swimming pool in one corner."

In 1928, the tower caught fire, and in less than six hours the building had become a smoldering ruin. Except for the inconvenient shortage of scientific space, no one missed the gloomy old building.

It is impossible to measure the impact that John Cleve Green had on education in the greater Princeton area. Born in Maidenhead (Lawrenceville) in 1800, his formal education did not include college training. The foundation of his wealth lay in the China trade, where he dealt in tea, textiles, and opium (then considered as respectable as tobacco is today). On his return to this country, he was involved in the burgeoning railroad companies. When he died in 1875, it was reported that one-third of the college's endowment had been contributed by him, but his philanthropy continued for several decades through the administration of his estate. His generosity more than quadrupled the main campus lands, provided five major buildings, furnished seed money to spur the rapid increase in library volumes, financed the salary of the first full-time librarian, underwrote the college deficit for a number of years, and established and endowed important new curricula which brought the college to university status. In addition, he made significant contributions and bequests to Princeton Theological Seminary. Lastly, funds from his estate founded Lawrenceville School, the first important "feeder school" for the college. How many other individuals can be credited with such a profound effect on secondary, college, and religious education in an area such as Princeton?

The Observatory, Princeton University, N.J.

Publisher: The Valentine & Sons Publishing Co., Ltd., NY, Card No. 202,141 * Manufacturer: The Valentine & Sons Publishing Co., Ltd., NY, Printed in Great Britain * Type: Colored, Undivided Back * Postmark: Not Used * Value Index: C

This fascinating structure, correctly called the Observatory of Instruction, stood on Prospect Avenue near Washington Road. Sadly, it was destroyed in the 1960s to be supplanted by the Woodrow Wilson School.

In the 1870s, when the college was searching for a new faculty member to direct the astronomy program, the Halstead Observatory was on the other side of the campus, but it did not have a telescope as yet. To lure Professor Charles A. Young away from Dartmouth College, Princeton not only promised to install a telescope, but it also agreed to provide a residence/teaching observatory. Apparently the working conditions convinced Professor Young to leave his native New Hampshire.

The house which once stood on the corner next to Professor Young was the home of Professor Cyrus F. Brackett, a pioneer in the new field of electrical engineering. As scientists, they were rather suspect to a faculty of diehard conservative Calvinists. Thus, the corner of Prospect Avenue and Washington Road was dubbed "Atheists' Corner."

The two professors must have been good friends. Professor Brackett, who had the first classroom with electric lights, built the first telephone line in Princeton. It stretched a full block from his office in the John C. Green School of Science to Dr. Young's observatory!

Professor Lyman Spitzer, Jr., and his family were the last residents of this home/observatory. The strategic location was perfect for their young children to set up an elaborate lemonade stand. One Saturday morning, daughter "Cozy" and her friend, Carol Beth, were busily vending their concoction and were sloshing the glasses in pails of soapy water and rinse water. A student customer looked at the yellow liquid in his glass and thoughtfully asked no one in particular, "I wonder if there are any calories in detergent?"

Just before the Spitzers were forced to move out of the house, the former Woodrow Wilson School (now Corwin Hall) was moved back from Washington Road to its present location behind the fountain. Mrs. Spitzer, an active Bryn Mawr College alumna sold space in her home to watch the move. At 50 cents per person, she raised 75 dollars for her local alumnae club. It must have been quite a sight to watch a large brick and stone classroom building slide by. Although preparation took considerable time, the actual move of several hundred feet was completed in one day.

100

Raphael Tuck & Sons undoubtedly "improved" this photograph. The flag, the lady with her parasol, and the nattily dressed gentlemen have been superimposed on the original. The lines on the grassy field in the foreground suggest that it may have been an informal football field, or even a grass tennis court.

Seventy-Nine Hall (as the building is officially known) was the twenty-fifth reunion gift of the Class of 1879. Since a member of the class, Woodrow Wilson, was President of the University at the time, it is not surprising that he chose the tower room for his office. From the windows on the far side, he had a beautiful view of the rapidly developing Prospect Avenue with its new residences and eating clubs.

PRINCETON UNIVERSITY. Class 1879 Dormitory.

Publisher: Raphael Tuck & Sons, London, England, Card No. 5662, "Prin. Univ." * **Manufacturer:** Raphael Tuck & Sons, London, England, Printed in Holland * **Type:** Colored, Undivided Back * **Postmark:** Not Used * **Value Index:** E

Built for use as a dormitory, its proximity to the clubs made it a popular choice among the students. By today's standards it provided fairly luxurious living. A handbook of that era said, "The suites consist of a study, in which is set an open fireplace, and two single bedrooms, separated from the study by a passage opening from the stair hall." In 1960, the building was converted to offices for academic departments.

As mentioned in the text describing Nassau Hall, the statues of the lions which had guarded the entrance to Nassau Hall were moved to Seventy-Nine Hall where they were replaced by the bronze tigers. They gazed down Prospect Avenue for many years until deterioration forced their removal.

Palmer Physical Laboratory, subsequently known as Palmer Laboratory and now Palmer Hall, was the first of the two great science buildings erected in 1908 and 1909 on Washington Road south of Prospect Avenue. During four decades, the Palmer family—father Stephen and son Edgar—were generous contributors to Princeton University. The laboratory was Stephen's gift to recognize the work of Professor Cyrus Fogg Brackett, the pioneer electrical engineer and founder of the School of Electrical Engineering. Palmer also participated in at least two small groups of alumni, which acquired and donated property that ultimately had enormous impact on both the university and the town. The first parcel was Springdale Farm, site of the golf course and the

Palmer Physical Laboratory, Princeton University.

Publisher: Van Marter, Princeton, NJ, Card No. 2480/11, 5399 * **Manufacturer:** Printed in Germany * **Type:** Colored, Divided Back * **Postmark:** Not Used * **Value Index:** D

Graduate College. The second was a 1906 acquisition on Nassau Street in the heart of town. Two decades later, after a number of complex real estate transactions, that seed blossomed into the Palmer Square development.

The new laboratory provided two acres of space for the Departments of Electrical Engineering and Physics. Today, it continues in use for physics instruction and houses the Program in Science in Human Affairs and Princeton-in-Asia.

Guyot Hall. Princeton University.

Publisher: H. M. Hinkson, Stationer, Princeton, NJ * Manufacturer: The Albertype Co., Brooklyn, NY * Type: Black and White, Divided Back * Postmark: Not Used * Value Index: E

The photograph shows the north facade of the other great science building, Guyot Hall. The size of the building can be judged by the almost indistinguishable figures of the three men on the walkway near the center of the picture. As with the Palmer Physical Laboratory, approximately two acres of instructional space, equally shared by the Departments of Biology and Geology, were provided. Part of the original planning was that the land from Guyot Hall to Lake Carnegie would be laid out in botanical gardens and an arboretum. Expanded requirements for buildings, athletic fields, and parking lots have doomed that concept.

Arnold Guyot, Princeton's Swiss-born first Professor of Geology and Geography, was also the founder of the E. M. Museum of Geology and Archaeology, later renamed the Natural History Museum. It was originally located in the Prayer Hall (now the Faculty Room) of Nassau Hall. When moved to the new Guyot Hall, it occupied the entire first floor, but over the years the need for academic space has superseded that of the museum.

One of the delightful features of Collegiate Gothic architecture was the liberal use of stone carvings, usually called gargoyles, for decoration. This architectural style was standard on the Princeton Campus for 50 years, and Guyot Hall holds the record for having the largest number of gargoyles. Although none are identifiable on the postcard because of the size of the building, there are approximately 200 of them in the stone trim. Because they are representations of animals, Guyot Hall has been termed "a veritable barnyard for gargoyles." Quite logically, living species of animals are represented on the biology wing of the building, and extinct animals on the geology wing.

McCosh Infirmary, Princeton University.
Princeton, N. J.

Publisher: Christie Whiteman, Princeton, NJ * Manufacturer: Probably Curt Teich Co., Chicago, IL, or Brooklyn Post Card Co., Inc., New York, NY * Type: Colored, Divided Back * Postmark: Not Used * Value Index: D

Sandwiched in between Palmer Physical Laboratory and Guyot Hall is the older Isabella McCosh Infirmary, built in 1893. The photograph shows that American publishers also enhanced their wares with superimposed features. Automobiles were novelties just before World War I, and the addition of the stylish two-seater motor car was probably a marketing ploy. Why is it on the lawn instead of the driveway?

When the college called James McCosh from Scotland to the presidency, it received an unexpected fringe benefit in the person of his wife, Isabella. The daughter of a famous physician, Mrs. McCosh displayed a profound interest in and practical knowledge of medicine. Known as "a woman of fine intellect and a notable sense of humor," she endeared herself to generations of students by her personal care when illness struck. She received a list of sick students every day and personally ministered to them in their rooms. She also wrote to their parents to assure them that their sons were being cared for. The town did not have a hospital, and Dr. McCosh, unquestionably backed by Mrs. McCosh, urged the trustees to establish an infirmary.

Five years after their retirement, the Isabella McCosh Infirmary opened its doors. An interesting aspect of this effort is the financial support supplied by faculty wives and other women connected with the university.

The illustration shows the building after at least two remodelings. The annex in the rear was added in 1899 to provide space to take care of students with contagious diseases. The dormer windows at the top of the building were added to create usable space in the attic.

With the growth of student enrollment, advances in the medical arts, and the founding of the Princeton Hospital, the original infirmary building became outmoded. In 1925, it was torn down and replaced by the present infirmary. A footnote to the history of the old building is that the bricks were salvaged to build a beautiful home a few blocks away on the southeast corner of Prospect Avenue and Harrison Street.

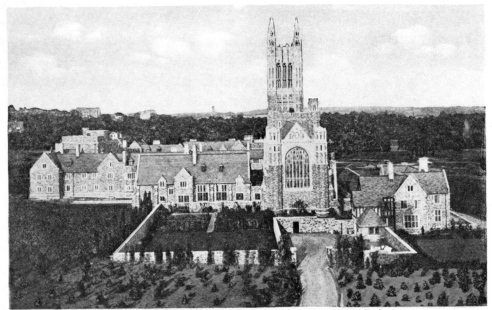

GRADUATE COLLEGE, CLEVELAND TOWER & WYMAN HOUSE, PRINCETON, N. J.

Publisher: Probably Christie Whiteman, Princeton, NJ * Manufacturer: Probably Curt Teich Co., Chicago, IL * Type: Colored, White Border, Divided Back * Postmark: Not Used * Value Index: E

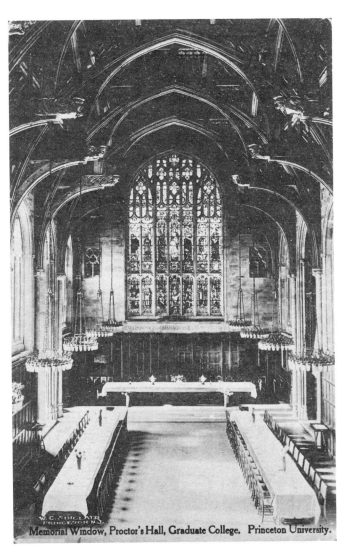

Memorial Window, Proctor's Hall, Graduate College. Princeton University.

Publisher: W. C. Sinclair, Princeton, NJ * Manufacturer: The Albertype Co., Brooklyn, NY * Type: Black and White, Divided Back * Postmark: October 11, 1917 * Value Index: E

This picture of the Graduate College complex was taken shortly after its dedication in 1913. The buildings obscure the view of the golf course; the main campus, and town lie to the left in the background. Aerial photographs were rare before World War I; from what vantage point was this scene photographed? A daring cameraman probably climbed the tall water tower which once stood behind the college to record this interesting panorama.

Cleveland Tower was financed by public subscription; because of its height (173 feet) and location on an uncluttered hillock, it dominates the Princeton skyline. Wyman House, at the lower right, is the residence of the Dean of the Graduate School. Princeton University carefully distinguishes between "Graduate School" and "Graduate College." The former refers to the curricular work of the graduate students, the latter to the living accommodations. In the beautiful buildings shown in the illustration, no classes are held. All course work is conducted in the classrooms, laboratories, and libraries on the main campus over a mile away. Bicycles have always been very popular among graduate students.

Reams of prose have been written about the monumental battle which raged for a dozen years between Woodrow Wilson and Andrew Fleming West, first Dean of the Graduate College, over the location of the new Graduate College. Although Wilson held the power and influence of his office, West was backed by the two most powerful trustees, Grover Cleveland and Moses Taylor Pyne. West won, the college was located away from the main campus, and Wilson's defeat signalled the beginning of the end of his career in academia. He answered the call of politics, which led him to the Governorship of New Jersey and the United States Presidency.

In its infancy, the Graduate College was housed on Bayard Lane in "Merwick," which is now a unit of the Medical Center at Princeton. Protocol for the evening meal was established at the beginning and was maintained with minor changes for the next half century. Academic gowns were always worn, and the meal was presided over by the resident faculty member. Wednesday dinners were special; evening clothes were worn under the gowns, the Dean was present, and there was a guest speaker. Remember, etiquette had formal rules, and college men had frequent need for formal clothes. It is probable that they wore their "soup and fish" attire more often than today's students wear neckties.

The illustration shows the new graduate dining room in Procter Hall (incorrectly identified as Proctor's Hall). It is not surprising that many individuals assume that it was built as a chapel. The theme of the beautiful stained glass window, however, is not biblical; appropriately for a Presbyterian-based University, it symbolizes Christian Learning.

William C. Procter, of Ivory Soap fame, pledged 2 million dollars toward the building of the Graduate College, and the strings he attached to the gift were a strong influence on the decision to build away from the main campus. In addition to donating Procter Hall, he helped to underwrite the other buildings in the complex and endowed thirteen fellowships. Finally, he gave the 1927 addition to the Graduate College.

The student who sent this Postcard to his girl in 1917 wrote, "I am still here, expecting a red card every time the letter carrier comes." Was he in academic difficulty, or did he expect a call from the war-time draft?

The Organ, Proctor's Hall,
Graduate College. Princeton University.

Publisher: W. C. Sinclair, Princeton, NJ * Manufacturer: The Albertype Co.,
Brooklyn, NY * Type: Black and White, Divided Back * Postmark: Not Used *
Value Index: E

Prospect Avenue,
Princeton, N. J.

Publisher: Christie Whiteman, Princeton, NJ, Card No. 6588 12E46 * Manufacturer: Made in Germany * Type: Colored,
Divided Back * Postmark: Mailed; No Postmark * Value Index: B

The photograph picturing the main entrance and organ of Procter Hall repeats the curious misspelling, "Proctor's Hall." It must have been an impressive sight to see a large group of men, dressed in their flowing black academic gowns, assemble for dinner in this Collegiate Gothic hall. In the spring, the late afternoon sun would light up the stained glass window. This medieval picture would be idyllic with organ music in the background.

Andrew Fleming West, founder and first Dean of the Graduate School, was not only a witty scholar and administrator, but he was also a genius at raising funds. Shortly after Procter Hall was built, he was showing Henry Clay Frick, the steel magnate, around the new Graduate College. When Frick criticized the new dining hall because it "Looked too damn much like a church—all it needs is an organ," West talked him into giving one. A four-manual organ was installed in the gallery in 1916 at a cost of $40,000. When you consider that a comfortable home could be purchased for a few thousand dollars, that was a major gift. The original organ was replaced in the 1960s.

Today, the organ is one of the hidden cultural treasures of Princeton University. Not only is it a beautiful musical instrument, but the acoustics are excellent. The size of the hall (36 by 108 feet), the vaulted ceiling, the paneled walls, and the stone floor combine with the organ to provide an inspirational music experience. When the University Chapel organ was shipped to England for overhaul, Procter Hall was again the home of the finest organ on campus.

This illustration of Prospect Avenue was a product of the prolific publisher of Princetoniana, Christie Whiteman. On the back side of the postcard, typed in purple ink, is the message, "The picture on the opposite side is of myself and a little girl 5 years old. Christie Whiteman, Princeton, N.J." Almost eighty years later his two daughters have that typewriter, and it continues in working order. The brick wall visible behind Mr. Whiteman and his friend enclosed University Field, where the football and baseball games were once played.

Prospect Avenue was first cut through the farm on the east side of Washington Road in 1877. Its convenient location near the campus made it popular among faculty members, who soon began to build comfortable homes at the site. Ivy Club built the first eating clubhouse on Prospect Avenue in 1883, and by the end of the 19th century, "The Street" (as it was familiarly called) was dominated by the eating clubs.

Most colleges and universities had fraternities and sororities to provide meals, social life, and housing for their undergraduate members, but the student life at the College of New Jersey evolved differently. The feeding of the students was always a thorny problem, and in 1856, the college solved it by closing the refectory. Thus, the students were forced to obtain their meals in the small country town. Eating clubs already existed, but they proliferated when the college facility closed. The clubs were small and short-lived, disappearing upon graduation of the group, but they were marked by exotic names, such as "Old Bourbon," "Hole in the Wall," and "Shucks." The fraternity movement was crushed by the college administration, but the eating clubs were, of necessity, tolerated. Ivy Club, the first self-perpetuating club, was founded in 1879. By World War I, 16 upperclass student eating clubs had been formed. It was reported that in 1914, almost 87% of the juniors and seniors were members of a club. The students have never resided in their club buildings.

This view looking west along the north side of Prospect Avenue was photographed circa 1905. Although enlarged and remodeled, the distinctive homes of Elm Club and Tiger Inn still serve their members today. In the distance, at the left of the picture, the blockish portico of the original Colonial Club is visible.

Elm Club, founded in 1895, had its beginning in a leased property on Bayard Lane. When the decision was made to build on Prospect Avenue, the members selected Moses Taylor Pyne's favorite architect with the interesting name of Raleigh C. Gildersleeve. Among his Princeton works were the Upper and Lower Pyne buildings on Nassau Street and McCosh Hall. Recently, Elm Club fell on hard

Publisher: Richard Rowland, Princeton, NJ, Card No. 162 * Manufacturer: National Art View Co., NY, Germany * Type: Black and White, Undivided Back * Postmark: Not Used * Value Index: E

times, precipitated by a drastic drop in membership. It has merged with two other troubled clubs to form the Dial-Elm-Cannon Club.

Tiger Inn had its roots in an ephemeral eating club located at the corner of Nassau and Chambers Streets, recently the location of Alan Royce Fine Clothing. The group moved to a rented house on William Street in 1890. The members simply called their place "The Inn," and the college mysteriously dubbed them "The Sour Balls." In less than two years, the club was formally incorporated as "The Tiger Inn" and moved to larger quarters in University Cottage, which stood at the end of University Place, or roughly in the middle of the present street by McCarter Theater. In 1895, a gala reception and dance celebrated the occupation of the new Tudor-style clubhouse.

The photographer for the previous postcard must have walked across the street to capture this view toward the east on the north side of Prospect Avenue. However, this sight is not familiar; the club buildings have disappeared long ago. On the porch in the foreground, note the five stylishly dressed students wearing suits, neckties, and straw "skimmers." It is also apparent that the street is in the early stages of its development. There is little or no shrubbery, the trees barely reach second floor levels, and a private home is visible on the far side of Cap and Gown Club.

The University Cottage Club building, with its two large front bays, was the first one built by and for the eating club. Cap and Gown Club built on the site of its first home; the original house was moved to Olden Street where Mudd Manuscript Library now stands.

Publisher: Richard Rowland, Princeton, NJ, Card No. 161 * Manufacturer: National Art View Co., NY, Germany * Type: Black and White, Undivided Back * Postmark: Not Used * Value Index: E

On the old postcards printed in Germany, typographical errors were quite common. Obviously, this caption should read "Cap & Gown Club" rather than "Cap & Crown Club." Judging by the modest growth of the trees and shrubbery, this photograph was taken not long after the preceding postcard. The membership must have quickly outgrown the clubhouse, for in a dozen years it was moved to another site to make room for a new and larger facility.

In a town where moving buildings seemed to be a normal way of life, the history of the original clubhouse, which had been moved to Olden Street, is interesting. Its size and location near the other clubs made it an ideal home for newly organized eating clubs. Over the years, no less than seven clubs began there, and one occupied it twice. No wonder it was known as "The Incubator."

Publisher: Not Indicated * Manufacturer: Made in Germany * Type: Colored, Divided Back * Postmark: November 4, 1907 * Value Index: E

The third building to house the Cap and Gown Club was the second of three clubhouses on "The Street" designed by Raleigh C. Gildersleeve. Before it was built in 1908, the members consulted with President Wilson, who was then embroiled in his controversial "Quad Plan" proposal, which would have abolished all of the eating clubs. Understandably, the President was cool to the idea. They then turned to Moses Taylor Pyne, who predicted that the trustees would reject President Wilson's proposal and that it would be safe to build. Mr. Pyne was correct, and this illustration shows the new clubhouse which echoes the Gothic architecture of the buildings then being added to the campus. The sparse vegetation indicates that the picture was taken soon after completion and before the landscaping was completed.

Publisher: McGown-Silsbee Litho Co., NY, Card No. 2578/3 * Manufacturer: McGown-Silsbee Litho Co., NY, Printed in Germany * Type: Colored, Divided Back * Postmark: June 30, 1916 * Value Index: D

The message on the back of the postcard provides a glimpse of the low-key tempo of campus life during the World War I era. A lady who was visiting Princeton University wrote to a friend in Middletown, New York, that her group ". . . had a delightful address of welcome from the President, a brief organ recital, and delicious refreshments served on the lawn." The President was of course, John Grier Hibben, the recital must have been in Marquand Chapel, and the refreshments were probably served next door on the lawn of Prospect.

Publisher: The Rotograph Co., New York City, Card No. 55316 * Manufacturer: The Rotograph Co., New York City, "Sol-Art Prints," Germany * Type: Colored, Undivided Back * Postmark: May 14, 1907 * Value Index: E

The date on which this postcard was addressed helps to pinpoint the publishing date. The new clubhouse was formally opened in June 1906. The background trees in leaf plus the time required to produce the postcard in Germany indicates that the photograph was taken near the opening date. The photograph had to be sent to Germany for printing in postcard format and returned to Princeton to be sold and mailed in May 1907. Note that the four-foot brick wall specified in the plans had not yet replaced the scrubby hedge in the foreground.

"The University Cottage Club" was the name adopted by the eight charter members of the second self-perpetuating eating club of the college. It had its roots in an informal eating group of freshmen with the descriptive name "The Seven Wise Men of Grease," which ate on the second floor of Dohm's, a saloon on Nassau Street across from the campus. The group moved to better facilities in the University Hotel, where the members decided to make the club permanent. Their first clubhouse was the leased University Cottage at the foot of Railroad Avenue (now University Place)—thus the club name. Within four years, they had purchased the current club site on Prospect Avenue and had built the large shingled house shown on another postcard. The quality of construction may have been questionable; within a dozen years, wear and tear inspired comments such as "cold as a barn" and "almost uninhabitable." Rather than repair or destroy it, the club purchased a lot and moved the building so that the new brick clubhouse could be built at the same location. The Tower Club must have thought the frame house was habitable, because it moved into the relocated clubhouse. For a year after the sale to the Tower Club, while waiting for their new quarters, the University Cottage Club members took their meals in the Princeton Inn and rented a room across the street in University Hall for their socializing.

This postcard is extremely unusual, because it shows the back of an eating club. The private tennis court was unique—so was the courtyard at the top of the steps. Imagine the impressive view the members enjoyed! Stretching below the courtyard was a panorama across sloping farmland, the shimmering water of the new Loch Carnegie (also dedicated in 1906), the Delaware and Raritan Canal, and looking towards the Pennsylvania Railroad main line at Princeton Junction.

The new University Cottage Club was unquestionably the most expensive and luxurious clubhouse built to that date. During construction it was called (perhaps enviously) "The White Elephant of Prospect Street." The club, however, was blessed with "Angels." The Palmers, father and son, probably

University Cottage Club, Princeton University, Princeton, N. J.

Publisher: Edward G. Van Marter, Princeton, NJ * **Manufacturer:** Made in Germany * **Type:** Colored, Divided Back * **Postmark:** Not Used * **Value Index:** E

the most generous contributors to the University during the early 20th century (Palmer Stadium, Palmer Laboratory, and Palmer Square), contributed an estimated three-quarters of the funds for the clubhouse.

An interesting bit of the Club's history is its relationship with Woodrow Wilson, who was elected an honorary member when he was a professor. As college president, he fought for his Quad Plan, which would have sounded the death knell for the clubs. Yet, he officially approved the plans for the new clubhouse, and during his tenure, he was a frequent speaker at club functions.

The wintry view in this illustration shows the original clubhouse on the property of the Campus Club. The location at the corner of Washington Road and Prospect Avenue must have had considerable appeal for the students. Among all of the clubs, it was the most accessible to the classrooms and laboratories of Seventy-Nine Hall, Dickinson Hall, the John C. Green School of Science, and the Chemical Laboratory. Before their new clubhouse replaced this building, the members had front row seats for the construction of the Palmer Physical Laboratory; also, McCosh and Guyot Halls across the street.

The home had been built by Andrew Fleming West, who lived there for a number of years before he became involved in the

Campus Club, Princeton, N. J.

Publisher: American News Co., NY, Leipzig, Berlin, Card No. A1494 * **Manufacturer:** American News Co., NY, Leipzig, Dresden, Berlin, "Excelsior" * **Type:** Black and White, Divided Back * **Postmark:** November 6, 1912 * **Value Index:** D

development of the Graduate College. To present day eyes, it was an impressive, comfortable mansion, but an architectural critic dismissed it as "an unimportant house." In 1909, to make room for the new clubhouse, the structure was moved to its present location on the southwest corner of Nassau Street and Princeton Avenue.

This was the third of the three club buildings, designed by Raleigh C. Gildersleeve. Although it resembles the Cap and Gown Club, completed a year before, it has no resemblance to the earlier Elm Club building. It is understandable that the design blends with the architecture of the university buildings which were then springing up across Washington Road. It is equally understandable that the clubs tried to out-do each other when they designed their houses. In the case of the Campus Club, one author said that the design attempted to "out-Gothicize" the recently completed Cap and Gown Club. Fortunately, the two clubhouses are a block apart.

Campus Club was the first eating club founded in the new century—1900. As six other clubs did, the members set up shop for a year or two in "The Incubator" on Olden Street across from the University Athletic Field. In 1902 the West property was acquired; the Club remains there today.

Publisher: Christie Whiteman, Princeton, NJ * Manufacturer: Not Indicated * Type: Sepia, Divided Back * Postmark: Not Used * Value Index: D

At the left of this photograph, almost concealed by the branches of the evergreen tree, is the base of the cannon which is the symbol of this club. As did many of the older eating clubs, the Cannon Club acquired a former private residence as its first permanent home on Prospect Avenue. The house had been built for Henry Fairfield Osborn, classmate of Moses Taylor Pyne and first Professor of Comparative Anatomy at the college. Several years before the club purchased the property, Professor Osborn had left Princeton to assume the Presidency of the Museum of Natural History in New York. The club occupied the house for a decade, but when the members were faced with major repairs to the structure, they opted to build a new clubhouse, and the Osborne house was razed.

Cannon Club. Princeton, N. J.

Publisher: American News Co., NY, Leipzig, Berlin, Card No. A1501 * Manufacturer: American News Co., NY, Leipzig, Dresden, Berlin * Type: Black and White, Undivided Back * Postmark: Not Used * Value Index: E

Cannon Club followed a familiar pattern. Founded in 1895, it was the third club to lease University Cottage at the foot of University Place. After two years it became the second resident of "The Incubator" on Olden Street for another pair of years, and then moved into the Osborn house in 1899. The new clubhouse was built in 1910.

The photograph for this post-card must have been taken at the time the new clubhouse was completed. There appears to be rubble in the front yard, there are no foundation plantings, and the blank windows indicate that it is not yet occupied. Also, there is no sign of the cannon; it must have been returned at a later date. Note that the fence in the foreground is the same one shown in the previous postcard. Later, a stone wall to match the house replaced the fence.

This clubhouse, built with the same local stone as many of the University buildings, served until the general decline in the eating club memberships during the 1960s. Lack of members forced it to close in 1972, and the building was sold to the University in 1974. It is now called Notestein Hall and houses the Office of Population Research.

Publisher: Princeton University Store, Princeton, NJ, Card No. AA5550 * Manufacturer: American News Co., NY, Leipzig, Dresden, Berlin, "Steeldructone," Made in Germany * Type: Black and White, Divided Back * Postmark: Not Used * Value Index: E

Cannon Club is not dead. In 1989, Dial Lodge, which was suffering from low membership, merged with Cannon Club. The Cannon Club was able to provide the needed working capital. The new eating club was the "Dial and Cannon Club." In 1990, another merger took place, when Elm Club was taken into the fold. The organization is now known as the Dial-Elm-Cannon Club.

The building illustrated on the postcard, with the imposing pillars and wide veranda, was the second home of the Charter Club. Interestingly, it was designed by an undergraduate, David Adler, Class of 1905. the clubhouse was constructed in 1903, therefore Mr. Adler must have been a teenager when he attacked such a major project. The general appearance is reminiscent of the huge beach-front "cottages" which dotted the New Jersey seashore at the turn of the 20th century.

The pattern for housing the club was a familiar one. Founded in 1901, it occupied "The Incubator" until this frame build-ing was erected on Prospect Avenue. When the members moved in, Charter Club's roll of thirty-seven undergraduates was the largest on "The Street." After pur-

Publisher: Edward G. Van Marter, Princeton, NJ * Manufacturer: Made in Germany * Type: Colored, Divided Back * Postmark: Not Used * Value Index: E

chasing the house next door, both buildings were sold and moved away when the new clubhouse was built in 1913. During con-struction, the members returned to "The Incubator."

At its inception, the membership of Charter Club was predominantly Philadelphian. Therefore, it was not surprising that a Philadelphia firm, Mellor and Meigs, was selected to design a new clubhouse; architect Arthur Meigs was a member of the club. Although the new stone building does not at all resemble the frame structure it replaced, note that the broad entrance steps and the design of the balustrade echo those of the earlier building. The Chestnut Hill stone is the same material used for Blair Hall, Stafford Little Hall, and other campus buildings. If "Chestnut Hill" refers to a nearby geographical source for the stone, it must represent another Philadelphia connection. A major residential section of that city bears the same name.

PRINCETON CHARTER CLUB, PRINCETON, N. J.

Publisher: Christie Whiteman, Princeton, NJ * Manufacturer: Probably Curt Teich Co., Chicago IL * Type: Colored, White Border, Divided Back * Postmark: Not Used * Value Index: E

Not long after the new clubhouse was opened, the turmoil of World War I struck. Many of the eating clubs closed their houses for the duration of the war, among them Charter Club. The members remaining on campus were invited to share the facilities of the University Cottage Club.

This strange-looking structure was the first permanent home of the Colonial Club after its early years in leased properties on Nassau Street. The building was purchased from the Ivy Club in 1897 when that club moved into a new home across the street. On this postcard, the gabled section at the right of the picture provides a glimpse of the appearance of the former Ivy Club building.

The clapboard addition tacked on the front of the existing building was another example of architectural design by an undergraduate student. The members must have been satisfied with his work, however, because Frank Stewart was again selected ten years later to design their new clubhouse. To make room, the old house was sold and moved several miles to

Colonial Club. Princeton. N. J.

Publisher: American News Co., NY, Leipzig, Berlin, Card No. A1502 * Manufacturer: American News Co., NY, Leipzig, Dresden, Berlin, "Excelsior" * Type: Black and White, Undivided Back * Postmark: Not Used * Value Index: D

the famous Walker-Gordon Milk Farm in Plainsboro, New Jersey. For the next 70 years, it housed the offices of the farm.

The decision to build a new clubhouse was forced on the Colonial Club. During a summer thunderstorm, a bolt of lightning burned a hole in the roof, and the choice was made to replace the building rather than repair it. As noted for other clubs, a tie to the old clubhouse was the use of the same style of column for the portico.

The development pattern for Colonial Club was completely different from the earlier clubs. The founding members sagaciously leased a house on Nassau Street next door to the relatively new Evelyn College for Women (now Evelyn Place). As one author dryly commented, the club "found its competitive position strengthened." The President of Evelyn College was not enchanted, however. He feared

Colonial Club   Princeton University

Publisher: Princeton University Store, Princeton, NJ * Manufacturer: The Albertype Co., Brooklyn, NY * Type: Sepia, Divided Back * Postmark: Not Used * Value Index: E

that the influx of young males in the neighborhood "meant the ruination of Evelyn." The opinion of Evelyn's student body, of course, was not solicited.

Under official pressure, the club was forced to move, but it leased quarters not too far away at 186 Nassau Street. The students probably never knew it, but their second home was originally the sanctuary of the Second Presbyterian Church. After many changes and a physical relocation on the lot, it serves as commercial offices.

Although Dial Lodge was founded in 1907, it did not have its own quarters until the members moved to the former Cap and Gown Clubhouse in 1909. Perhaps the founders merely formalized their status at "White's Private Eating Establishment," where they had taken their meals since their freshmen year, 1905-1906. After purchasing a lot on Prospect Avenue, the clubhouse shown in this illustration was built in 1917.

Dial Lodge was unquestionably the child of Woodrow Wilson's controversial "Quad Plan" (sometimes known as the "Quad Wrangle Plan"). In the first decade of this century criteria for membership in the eating clubs were heavily weighted toward family wealth and social standing. Dial members had not been elected to

Dial Lodge
Princeton University

Publisher: Princeton University Store, Princeton, NJ * Manufacturer: The Albertype Co., Brooklyn, NY * Type: Sepia, Divided Back * Postmark: November 23, 1927 * Value Index: E

the existing clubs, therefore the founders were not in favor of the word "club." Woodrow and Ellen Wilson encouraged the formation of Dial Lodge; they even invited the members to a dance at Prospect. President Wilson lost his "Quad Plan" battle, but the exclusivity of the eating clubs has continued to trouble Princeton University.

As mentioned in the description of Cannon Club, in 1989, Dial Lodge merged with the defunct Cannon Club to form Dial and Cannon Club. In 1990, the new organization merged once more, this time with Elm Club. The current name is Dial-Elm-Cannon Club.

Ivy Club, Princeton, N. J.

Publisher: American News Co., NY, Leipzig, Dresden, Berlin, Card No. C3793, 120466 * Manufacturer: American News Co., NY, Leipzig, Dresden, Berlin, "Litho-Chrome," Germany * Type: Colored, Divided Back * Postmark: June 2, 1910 * Value Index: E

Although Ivy Club is the oldest of the self-perpetuating eating clubs, it was the subject of comparatively few early postcards. Neither of its first two homes is represented on a postcard, because the club was already settled in its present house before the postcard era began.

The pattern of the club's development is a familiar one, but it is interesting to see how events molded the club into the proto-type for the eating club system. A key point to remember is that interclass rivalries were so intense during the 19th century that social mixing among classes was minimal.Also, eating arrangements were haphazard and difficult. The "History of the Ivy Club 1879-1929" records that in 1876, when the 97 members of the Class of 1880 arrived, ". . .there were few places to obtain food. These consisted of one restaurant, a number of boarding houses, a newly erected Commons and the University Hotel." A group of "the leading men of the class, particularly the athletes" ate together at a reserved table in the Commons, but were asked to leave during their second year, probably because of a food fight. The boarding houses were booked solid, and to resolve the crisis, it was decided to "buy a stove, hire a cook and set up a table in a room of Ivy Hall which was then vacant." The sixteen members of the informal association called themselves the "Ivy Hall Eating Club."

The students quickly discovered that some type of organization was required to operate an eating facility. The group functioned well for over a year, but in 1879, some members dropped out of college and were replaced by invitation. The last step toward establishing a continuing organization was when "finally, certain '81 men (Juniors) were invited to set up a separate table."

Ivy Hall had been privately built to house the short-lived (1847-1852) Law School. It later served as headquarters for the D & R Canal Company before being owned by Trinity Episcopal Church. The club moved to its own house on Prospect Avenue in 1882. The building underwent a major remodeling in 1888. When the club moved into its present house in 1899, the property was sold to Colonial Club.

Thus Ivy Club was not only the first self-perpetuating eating club, but it also inadvertently set the precedent of membership limited to juniors and seniors. In addition, it pioneered in establishing Prospect Avenue as the locale for the eating clubs. A history of the period comments that, "Prospect Street was then a mere country road without sidewalks or pavements, the path now known as McCosh Walk was ankle-deep in mud during bad weather and Ivy was regarded as venturesome in moving so far from the College."

Unlike many of the eating clubs, Key and Seal Club had only two homes during its 64 years of existence. The comfortable-looking frame house shown in the photograph was the first clubhouse. It was occupied from the club's founding in 1904 until the building was moved away from the site in 1924 to make room for the new clubhouse. Key and Seal Club closed in 1968, when the club system was once more under heavy fire. Princeton University purchased the building; it is now part of the Stevenson Halls complex, a nonselective undergraduate study, dining, and social facility. This complex was named for Adlai E. Stevenson, Class of 1922, who twice ran for the Presidency of the United States against General Dwight D. Eisenhower.

Publisher: Princeton University Store, Princeton, NJ, Card No. AA5558 * Manufacturer: American News Co., NY, Leipzig, Dresden, Berlin, "Steeldructone," Made in Germany * Type: Sepia, Divided Back * Postmark: Not Used * Value Index: D

The situation for this postcard is the opposite to that for the Ivy Club. There is a postcard illustrating the earlier clubhouse, but none for the later one. Eating club postcards went out of fashion in the 1920s.

This postcard of Quadrangle Club's first permanent home shows one of the many well-travelled structures in Princeton. It had been built by Professor Henry Burchard Fine on the south side of Prospect Street, but Ivy Club moved it to the north side when its own clubhouse was built. The Quadrangle Club, founded in 1901, purchased the building, then moved it again across Prospect Street to where Tower Club now stands. Later, it had another move, this time away from the campus area.

Professor Fine was not only a world-renowned mathematician, but as Dean of the Faculty, he was a key figure in Woodrow Wilson's program to strengthen the faculty, inaugurate the preceptorial system, and overhaul the

Publisher: Van Marter, Princeton, NJ * Manufacturer: Not Indicated * Type: Black and White, Divided Back * Postmark: January 21, 1908 * Value Index: B

curriculum. One task which he could not have enjoyed was that of dismissing those students who did not meet the new, and more stringent, academic requirements.

When "Ida" sent this Postcard to inquire about a mislaid sewing pattern, she was not aware that a 1907 change in the law permitted the writing of the message on the address side. The manufacturer had delineated a message space, but she did not use it.

Without knowing it, the Quadrangle Club was attracted to Princeton's "travelling" houses. When it outgrew its quarters in Dean Fine's former home, the club purchased the beautiful building shown in this illustration. It had been the retirement home of James McCosh, President of the College of New Jersey. He had planned and supervised its construction in 1887 to prepare for his move from Prospect (the President's residence) in 1888. After his death in 1894, his widow lived in it until her death in 1909. The Quadrangle Club occupied the building from 1910 until construction on its new clubhouse began in 1916. The structure was sold, and the new owner moved it in two sections to a large plot on Nassau Street between Markham Road and Wilton Street.

Publisher: Princeton University Store, Princeton, NJ, Card No. AA5561 * Manufacturer: American News Co., NY, Leipzig, Dresden, Berlin, "Steeldructone," Made in Germany * Type: Sepia, Divided Back * Postmark: Not Used * Value Index: D

In recent years, the building was once more saved from destruction by moving it. Architect Robert Hillier recognized its historic importance to Princeton by moving it to the corner of the plot of land it occupied on Nassau Street, thereby making room for the condominiums which now stand there.

As World War I was devastating Europe, the Quadrangle Club was preparing to build its new clubhouse. The members selected an architect who was already active in Princeton, Henry O. Milliken, Class of 1905. By the time the United States became embroiled in the war in 1916, the new building was under construction on the site formerly occupied by the McCosh house. During the war period, the Quadrangle members were welcomed at the Cottage Club located two doors away. It must have been a beneficial arrangement for both clubs; the Quadrangle Club was homeless, and all of the clubs were feeling the pinch of drastically reduced enrollment.

Critics of architecture have

Publisher: C. E. Van Marter, Princeton, NJ, Card No. A-85449 * Manufacturer: Curt Teich Co., Chicago, IL, "C. T. American Art," Made in U.S.A. * Type: Colored, White Border, Divided Back * Postmark: Not Used * Value Index: E

not been enthusiastic over the present clubhouse. One comment was that "The doorway is totally out of scale with the rest of the facade, making the front look more awkward than it otherwise would." The Princeton Architectural Survey (1980) calls it a "Pretty pedestrian colonial revival." The building has obviously survived these criticisms.

In 1904, following the footsteps of several predecessors, the new Terrace Club began operation in "The Incubator" on Olden Street. The Club apparently had an excellent start. In its first year, there were 26 members, which compared favorably with the average of 30 for the thirteen clubs in existence at that time. Two years later, the club acquired the spacious residence shown in the illustration. It had belonged to Professor John Grier Hibben, who later succeeded Woodrow Wilson as President of Princeton University. Professor Hibben had built a new home on Washington Street (now Washington Road) on the slope of the hill behind the home of Professor Andrew Fleming West, currently the site of the Campus Club. Members lolling on the spacious side porch at the right of the

Publisher: Princeton University Store, Princeton, NJ, Card No. AA5560 * Manufacturer: American News Co., NY, Leipzig, Dresden, Berlin, "Steeldructone," Made in Germany * Type: Sepia, Divided Back * Postmark: November 21, 1911 * Value Index: E

picture must have had a marvelous view down Washington Street, across the large swampy area along the Stony Brook, toward the Brunswick Pike (now U.S. Route #1). They had ringside seats to watch the logging and excavation of the area, as well as the construction of the bridge to span the new lake. For a small country town, creation of the 400-acre lake was a vast project; practically all of the back-breaking work was performed by men and mules. Building the lake must have provided a welcome diversion for an undergraduate student body of approximately 1,200 students.

Technically, this 1920s postcard falls outside of our targeted period of 1900-1920, but after a year's absence, the Terrace Club members had moved back into their building during the 1920-1921 academic year. As one member related the chain of events, ". . . just as Terrace decided to demolish the house (to build a new one) the United States set out to demolish Germany—this saved the house." The club had retained an architect, had approved plans for a new clubhouse, and had been soliciting funds. When the United States entered World War I, the building campaign was called off, and the contributions were returned to the donors. After the armistice, it was decided to remodel rather than rebuild, probably based on

TERRACE CLUB, UNIVERSITY OF PRINCETON, PRINCETON, N. J.

Publisher: C. E. Van Marter, Princeton, NJ, Card No. A-94570 * Manufacturer: Curt Teich Co., Chicago, IL, "C. T. American Art," Made in U.S.A. * Type: Colored, White Border, Divided Back * Postmark: Not Used * Value Index: E

the wartime shortages and restrictions. Work commenced immediately. While construction moved ahead during the 1919-1920 school year, the members took their meals in a private dining room at the Nassau Inn. When the picture of the remodeled clubhouse is compared to the original, it is hard to believe that it is the same building.

Terrace Club holds two minor distinctions in the long history of the eating clubs. It is the only club which occupies the first clubhouse it purchased, and it is the only club which never had a Prospect Avenue address.

119

TOWER CLUB, PRINCETON UNIVERSITY, PRINCETON, N. J.

Publisher: C. E. Van Marter, Princeton, NJ, Card No. A-85451 * Manufacturer: Curt Teich Co., Chicago, IL, "C. T. American Art," Made in U.S.A. * Type: Colored, White Border, Divided Back * Postmark: December 30, 1930 * Value Index: E

Tower Club has had more homes than any of the other eating clubs. It began in 1902 in the "Monastery" (sometimes known as the "Bachelors Club"), a college-owned building made famous by the number of unmarried faculty members who lived there both before and after its occupation by the club. With a natural desire to be closer to the other eating clubs, Tower Club moved within the year to "The Incubator," "the `cradle' which had rocked so many infant clubs." When Cottage Club moved its old clubhouse to 89 Prospect Street to make room for its new home, Tower Club purchased the building in 1904. During the club's seven-year occupancy, it enlarged the property, repaired the building, and added a tennis court. In 1911, Quadrangle Club put the old Fine House on the market, and Tower Club bought it, because it was closer to the campus. The new Cloister Inn Eating Club purchased the vacated building.

Soon after, the members began to prepare plans for a new clubhouse. The layouts of every other club were analyzed with the expressed objective to have a clubhouse "designed first to be practical, then comfortable, then artistic without ostentation." Not having any financial "angels," they insisted on accumulating a solid nest egg before building. In 1916, the old Fine House was sold and moved to Nassau Street. Until they moved into the new clubhouse in 1917, the members had temporary quarters on Nassau Street over Marsh and Burke's Drug Store. When the war began, the drop in undergraduate enrollment was offset by serving officers who were in training on the campus and by sharing the new facility with the Terrace Club.

On April Fool's Day of 1921, a major fire broke out in the tower. Fortunately, the club's insurance completely covered all the loss, and the members expressed their gratitude to the Walter B. Howe and O. H. Hubbard Insurance Agencies. A point of interest is that the two agencies merged 40 years later and are still in business as Walter B. Howe, Inc.

During the peak usage of postcards, drawings and paintings of beautiful women were extremely popular. With the student population of the colleges and universities overwhelmingly male, the postcard industry was happy to supply this ready-made market. A favorite merchandising ploy was to produce sets of six, ten, or twelve cards. These were frequently packaged in an envelope to increase the unit sales from a few pennies to perhaps twenty-five cents. The postcard illustrated here was published as one in a set of six. Presumably, the other five were all painted by the same artist, John Bergman.

Although women in this era were beginning to be more active in sports, their participation in competitive athletics was probably limited to a lady-like game of tennis or golf. This striking postcard has a cherry red background to emphasize the traditional Princeton orange and black. Undoubtedly, the postcard was considered to be a bit naughty, because the young lady's limb was depicted.

Mr. Bergman would have been surprised to know that he unwittingly anticipated coeducation at Princeton University by 64 years.

Publisher: Copyrighted by J. Bergman, 1905 * Manufacturer: Illustrated Postal Card Co., NY * Type: Colored, Undivided Back * Postmark: Not Used * Value Index: B

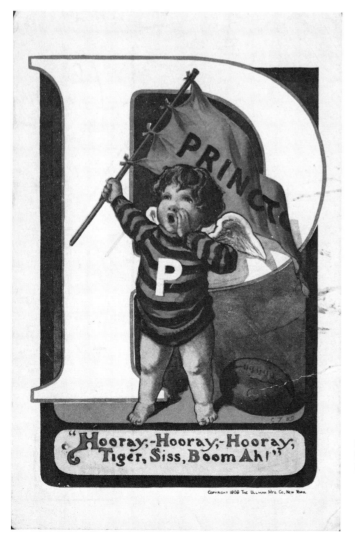

"Hooray,-Hooray,-Hooray, Tiger, Siss, Boom Ah!"

The unknown artist who drew this postcard was appealing to several segments of potential customers. Children were always a popular subject. By integrating a chubby cherub with the love of alma mater and the appeal of football, the postcard should have enjoyed excellent sales.

When "Clara" sent the Postcard to her friend, "Julia" in 1909, she apologized for writing it in her school-girl German. Translated, she said, "I do not believe that you met a man from Princeton, therefore I send you one. Your loving friend." Her postscript casts doubt on "Julia's" fluency in the language by offering to supply a translation if it is needed.

Publisher: American Post Card, "Colorgravure," Card Series No. 138, Subject No. 2454 * Manufacturer: Ullman Manufacturing Co., NY (Copyright 1909) * Type: Colored, Divided Back * Postmark: October 2, 1909 * Value Index: A

This is another postcard of a frisky tiger drawn by the mysterious "S .P .S." or "S .P .C.". It is difficult to be certain because of the way he inscribed his initials. All of his postcards were simple two-color printing (orange and black, of course) on inexpensive card stock. For this postcard, only the dog's bandages, the tiger, and the football are colored orange.

In this era, Princeton, Yale, and Harvard were the national powers in football. The first of Walter Camp's All-American Teams included only players from these three schools. The Princeton-Yale rivalry was so intense that if Princeton won ten games in an eleven-game schedule, the overall season was considered

Publisher: Van Marter, Princeton, NJ * Manufacturer: Not Indicated * Type: Colored, Divided Back * Postmark: Not Used * Value Index: B

to be a loss if Yale won the eleventh game. Unfortunately, from 1900 until the football season was virtually eliminated by World War I, Yale won twelve games, there were three ties, and Princeton won only twice. The Yale bulldog did not have occasion to cry very often during those years.

At the turn of the century, magazines and newspapers were dependent on artists to draw the illustrations for their publications. Among the famous illustrators were Howard Chandler Christy, James Montgomery Flagg, and Charles Dana Gibson. Equally famous was Richard Felton Outcault, who drew the cartoons for the first colored comic supplement to a Sunday newspaper. Mr. Outcault was also the inadvertent father of the phrase "Yellow Journalism." One of his cartoon characters was called "The Yellow Kid," but the newspaper had difficulties with the printing of yellow. The dazzling shade selected caught the fancy of the public, and evolved into the phrase used for the journalistic style we now find in supermarket tabloids.

Publisher: J. Ottman Lith. Co., NY (Copyright 1905) * Manufacturer: J. Ottman Lith. Co., NY * Type: Colored, Undivided Back * Postmark: Not Used * Value Index: A

In another context, this postcard could be interpreted as a social commentary on the sport of football. At the time of publication, mass plays were then at the heart of the game. Injuries were frequent, there were fatalities, and there were movements to ban football. At the request of President Theodore Roosevelt, however, the rules were revised to make the game safer. One major change was to permit the forward pass.

122

This photograph of the Class of 1887 Boat House is one of those rare postcards which depicts a building being used. At the edge of the water, eight oarsmen hold a shell over their heads prior to putting it in the water. There are also about thirty men (with hats and overcoats) milling around on the dock behind the coach's launch, and four touring automobiles are randomly parked next to the building. There is no clue to identify the occasion; perhaps there was a regatta in progress.

The twenty-fifth reunion gift from the Class of 1887 was announced in 1912, and the building was ready for alumni inspection on the 1913 Alumni Day. Oddly enough, although the lake was new, this is the second

Publisher: Not Indicated * Manufacturer: Not Indicated * Type: Photograph, Divided Back * Postmark: Not Used * Value Index: B

boat house built for Princeton Rowers. In 1874, in front of a large group of students and "ladies and gentlemen from New York", President McCosh had dedicated a large boat house on the bank of the D & R Canal. Dodging the traffic of boats and barges was not only difficult, but was dangerous as well. Competitive rowing was suspended in 1884 and was not revived until the new lake provided an appropriate stage for a rowing program.

As a postscript to the aborted early program, the first boat house followed the time-honored pattern of many Princeton buildings. It was moved to the other side of Carnegie Lake, where it then served as a canoe house until the mid-20th century.

Unquestionably, the photograph for this postcard was taken after the conclusion of a race. In the shell at the center of the postcard, the men appear to be resting on their oars, and the smaller boats certainly would not be there if a race was in progress. Finally, close examination reveals that the solid dark horizontal line bisecting the picture is composed of hundreds of spectators standing on the bank. The original rowing program was conducted under the aegis of the Princeton Boating Club, and the costs were largely borne by the participants. For example, the shells (often made of paper) were purchased by the students themselves. At the first intercollegiate regatta in which the college competed, the freshmen crew surprised the rowing world by winning its race.

University Crew on Loch Carnegie, Princeton, N. J.

Publisher: McGown-Silsbee Litho Co., NY, Card No. 2578/7, 1440 * Manufacturer: McGown-Silsbee Litho Co., NY, Printed in Germany * Type: Colored, Divided Back * Postmark: Not Used * Value Index: C

Unfortunately, that was the only win a Princeton crew recorded in the 19th century. After the new lake was dedicated in 1906, the Princeton University Rowing Association was organized. At first, competition was solely intramural, largely because President Woodrow Wilson was not in favor of any expansion of the athletic program. From the faculty, Dr. J. Duncan Spaeth, Professor of English and former Captain of the University of Pennsylvania rowing crew, was drafted by the students to coach the crews. In 1911, the year after President Wilson's resignation, Princeton returned to the intercollegiate rowing scene. In his more than 15 years of volunteer coaching, Dr. Spaeth brought his crews to the forefront of the sport.

Since the middle of the 19th century, tennis has been a most popular sport played by the Princeton students. Organized play began in 1882 with the formation of the Princeton Lawn Tennis Association. Because the college did not have its own courts, the students used those of a local club at the foot of Chambers Street. Construction of the courts shown on this Postcard was begun in 1895. The eight courts shown here were matched by a similar group located off the right of the picture.

Today, it is hard to visualize such a wide open area on the main campus. The photographer is facing Washington Road with Palmer Physical laboratory to his left and Guyot Hall to his right. Barely visible in the center is the

Tennis Courts, Princeton University.

Publisher: Van Marter, Princeton, NJ * Manufacturer: H. Wessler * Type: Sepia, Divided Back * Postmark: October 14, 1913 * Value Index: C

original Isabella McCosh Infirmary. In 1959, the Princeton Alumni Weekly announced a building program with the statement, "The new quadrangle contains housing, dining, library, and recreational facilities for more than 500 undergraduates, situated in the tennis court area between the infirmary and Patton Hall." The five new buildings, completed in 1961, are the core of Wilson College. All of the campus tennis courts are centralized on Brokaw Field between Dillon Gymnasium and Hobart Baker Memorial Rink.

Princeton University has a glittering tennis history. Until the end of the Postcard Golden Age, Princeton had a host of intercollegiate champions and three undefeated teams. The next two decades produced another group of champions and eight undefeated teams. The enthusiasm has been communicated to the town; the Princeton Community Tennis Program has been used as a model for local programs throughout the United States.

This photographic postcard and the subsequent postcard of University Field clearly illustrate the importance of baseball to Princeton University at the turn of the 20th century. The permanent seating was configured for the baseball diamond, and the crowd shown in this illustration provides proof that our national pastime was a very popular collegiate sport. Photographic postcards are frequently difficult to date, because comparatively few of them were mailed, the backs had an almost generic quality, and there were seldom any printed clues. In this photograph, note that most of the men are wearing suits and straw hats. The only woman who is clearly visible wears a dress down to her shoetops. For those who have noticed that the roof over the seats behind homeplate is gone, the roof was eliminated by a fire. The best guess at the date of this postcard is the early 1920s.

Publisher: Not Indicated * Manufacturer: Not Indicated * Type: Photograph, Divided Back * Postmark: Not Used * Value Index: B

This comfortable-looking building, with its picket fence and welcoming gate, was originally named the University Athletic Club. It was donated by Henry Fairfield Osborn (1877), world-famous scientist, who later became Professor of Comparative Anatomy. Built in 1892, it quickly acquired a new name, the Osborn Club House. Situated in the southwest corner of University Field, it provided training quarters for athletic teams. When sports were concentrated in the Palmer Memorial Stadium area, the building became the Third World Center. This photograph was taken before 1911, because in that year construction of the Ferris Thompson Gateway on Prospect Avenue replaced the pickets with the present brick fence.

Publisher: Van Marter, Princeton, NJ * Manufacturer: Not Indicated * Type: Black and White, Divided Back * Postmark: Not Used * Value Index: B

In the entrance hall, formerly the trophy room, a stone over the fireplace is engraved "Oranje Boven." Translated from Dutch, it says "Orange Above All." It was the battlecry of the troops of William III, House of Nassau (for whom Nassau Hall was named), who was also Prince of Orange. Thus, a Dutch patriotic expression is peculiarly appropriate for the athletic teams of an American university.

University Field was located on the land now occupied by the Engineering Quadrangle. In 1876 a mass meeting of the college was called to discuss the fact that the team's leased playing fields would no longer be available. At the meeting, William Libbey, Jr., Class of 1877, proposed the solution which served the baseball, football, and track programs for more than eighty-five years. The University Hotel Co., whose hostelry stood on the east corner of Nassau Street and University Place (then Railroad Avenue), would lease land on Prospect Street to the college and would "Fit it up with a quarter-mile course and a first-class ball field." The fact that William Libbey, Sr., was a founding director of the hotel company did not impede the rental negotiations.

Publisher: Christie Whiteman, Princeton, NJ, Card No. 6585 12 E 46 * Manufacturer: Made in Germany, Printed in Germany * Type: Colored, Divided Back * Postmark: Not Used * Value Index: B

As football became the preeminent spectator sport, temporary stands were installed on all four sides of the gridiron to accommodate the crowds; the stands shown in this illustration were not used. The year 1905 had to be a peak in the history of the field. A crowd of 25,000 people descended on the little town to see the Army-Navy football game. President Theodore Roosevelt and his entourage were entertained by Princeton University President Woodrow Wilson prior to the game. The two service academies were assigned 15,000 seats, and the others were sold to Princeton alumni, staff, and students. The proceeds from the latter were contributed to the Army and Navy Relief Societies.

Palmer Memorial Stadium - Princeton University

Publisher: Princeton University Store, Princeton, NJ * Manufacturer: The Albertype Co., Brooklyn, NY * Type: Sepia, Divided Back * Postmark: Not Used * Value Index: C

The scene on this postcard must have been photographed from an airplane at the time Palmer Memorial Stadium was completed. Areas for parking 3,200 automobiles were planned for the fields to the right, and pedestrian access appears to be rudimentary. At the top of the picture, the open land clearly shows how the town was concentrated along Nassau Street. The next line of buildings, the Prospect Avenue eating clubs, separate University Field from the new sports facility. Just beyond the curve of the horseshoe are the Nurses' Home (For McCosh Infirmary Staff) and the brand new 1911 Football Team Field House.

On April 1, 1914, it was announced that Edgar Palmer (1903) had contributed funds to build a stadium in memory of his father (who had given Palmer Physical Laboratory). The new field house was to be financed from funds donated by Cyrus H. McCormick (1879) to memorialize the undefeated 1911 football team. Both the stadium and the new field house were ready for use in less than seven months following the initial announcement! The Princeton Alumni Weekly bragged that a "convenient feature, and one which no other stadium possesses, is a large equipment of toilet rooms for both men and women." Perhaps the stadium was built too quickly; major structural repairs had to be made within the next decade.

In the first game played in the new stadium, Dartmouth was defeated. However, the Princeton team lost to Harvard, tied Amherst, and then lost to Yale on the day of the official dedication. It was not a good year for Princeton football, although there was an important long-term result. The anguished uproar from the alumni finally eliminated volunteer "coaching by committee," and a paid coach was hired.

On November 14, 1914—Dedication Day—the structure's capacity of 41,000 was almost filled by a crowd of 36,500 fans. Interestingly, Washington Road, the principal access road for vehicles, was closed from Prospect Avenue to the lake. Remember, however, that 1914 was the twilight of the pedestrian age; most of the alumni and visitors arrived by train. The Pennsylvania Railroad issued a special timetable for the extra trains. It included a detailed map to give the passengers walking routes to the stadium from the four railroad yards south of Blair Hall.

Historically, the true center of the campus for the students was the Big Cannon buried muzzle-down directly behind Nassau Hall. Referring to the cannon, one author said, "About it, some September night soon after the opening of College, is held the `rush,' the annual battle between the Freshmen and the Sophomores; here also are built the big fires which mark notable victories in football and baseball; and around it at Commencement time the Seniors gather for their last class exercises. It is the great totem of the place and about it the life of a Princeton undergraduate begins and ends."

Traditionally, when a victory called for a bonfire, signs were posted with the succinct message, "Freshmen Get Wood." One alumnus reminisced by saying that a football fire "was something to warm the cockles of everybody's heart. The team was pleased because it had ended a season in fitting manner. The upperclassmen were pleased because they didn't have to get wood. The freshmen were pleased because getting wood meant tearing down fences. And the owners of the fences were pleased because the University always replaced the fences with new ones and assessed the Freshmen."

The illustration shows at least ten young men piling the assorted lumber and boxes over the Cannon. Before the fire was started, the height of the stack must have been thirty feet or more. After oil, tar, and other flammables were added, the campus would have been as bright as day when the fire was at its fullest.

Bon Fire at Cannon, Princeton University.

Publisher: Van Marter, Princeton, NJ, Card No. 2489/22, 5410 * Manufacturer: Printed in Germany * Type: Colored, Divided Back * Postmark: April 10, 1914 * Value Index: C

Yale and Princeton

If this postcard depicts a Princeton-Yale football game, the site is a mystery. Most certainly, Princeton does not boast of a hill resembling the one behind the goal posts, and it is doubtful that New Haven has one. The best guess is that this is an early example of the generic postcard. Manufacturers could (and did) save on their production costs by printing a nice-looking neutral scene which could be overprinted with a caption suited to the special needs of a customer. If the consumers were willing to buy the item, manufacturers were willing and happy to supply it.

Publisher: Illustrated Postal Card Co., NY, Card No. 185.-2 * Manufacturer: Illustrated Postal Card Co., NY, Printed in Germany * Type: Colored, Divided Back * Postmark: July 13, 1908 * Value Index: B

Publisher: Not Indicated * Manufacturer: Not Indicated * Type: Photograph, Divided Back * Postmark: Not Used * Value Index: C

Although this photographic postcard does not have any printed identification on the back, the picture was unquestionably taken in Palmer Stadium after a Princeton-Yale football game. Customarily, the spectators would throng onto the playing field at the close of the game. At the right border are Yale cheerleaders in white sweaters. The one at the extreme right is carrying his megaphone over his shoulder. Except for the lady in the foreground, all of the visible individuals appear to be males, properly dressed in suits, hats, and neckties. Could there have been a melee around the goal posts, or was it just a festive crowd milling around on the field?

It is difficult to evaluate the success of Princeton football during the first two decades of the 20th century. World War I curtailed the schedule to a total of five games against service teams in 1917 and 1918. The rules of the game underwent major changes as well. For example, from 1903 to 1910, longitudinal lines at five-yard intervals changed the gridiron to a checkerboard, because the new rule permitting the quarterback to run the ball specified that he could not cross the scrimmage line less than five yards away from where the ball went into play. The rule change to permit forward passing did not permit the ball to be thrown across the scrimmage line or the goal line. Certain customs of that period had their impact on the team records as well. In the years when nine, ten, or eleven games were scheduled, they were crammed into six weeks. Also, it was the custom to play small schools in the first two or three scheduled games. This had the two-fold results of giving the team practice under actual game conditions and helping to create an excellent won-lost record.

Eliminating the two war years, the overall Princeton statistics were phenomenal with 85 percent won in a total of 162 games! After a disagreement over rules, Harvard was dropped from the schedule; however, the games with Harvard were restored in 1911. From 1901 to 1920, Princeton played its two bitterest rivals, Yale and Harvard a total of twenty-six times, and the team managed to win only five games—a puny record of less than 20 percent! Despite the good overall record, the alumni were unhappy.

Special purpose postcards such as the one shown were frequently sold during the Golden Age of Postcards. They provided a fast and easy communication of the score for that all-important game. This one must have been sent by a Yale alumnus, because his message was, "It was a great day."

The picture of the team is unusual for the era, because it shows over 50 players. Usually, team pictures included less than 30 men. This one is probably an early photograph of the entire squad so that the postcard could be printed and distributed before the season began.

The white-shirted player in the center was Edward Aloysius Dillon, the team captain. Although he was an All-American quarterback, his team was the

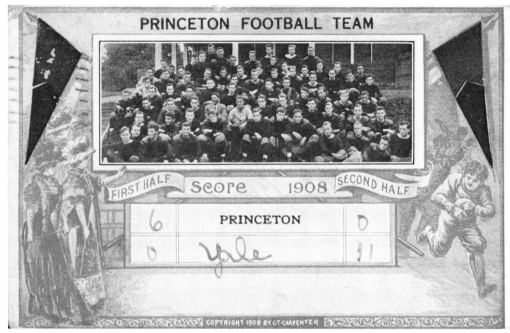

Publisher: C. T. Carpenter * Manufacturer: Not Indicated * Type: Black and White, Colored Inserts, Divided Back * Postmark: November 16, 1908 * Value Index: A

lowest-scoring and had the worst record of any Princeton team before 1923. The team registered five wins, but had three scoreless ties and lost the last two games to Dartmouth and Yale.

As a Sophomore in 1906, Captain Dillon had been quarterback on an undefeated Princeton team lead by Herbert Lowell Dillon (no relation) for whom Dillon Gymnasium was later named. It was the first season that forward passing was legal, and "Eddie" Dillon threw two scoring passes in the opening game against Villanova. If not the first, he must have been in the forefront of the quarterbacks to successfully use this new weapon.

Simple greeting cards with the seal of a college or university were frequently published in the early days of postcards. This postcard was engraved in orange, black and gold. The Princetonian who sent it to a young Miss vacationing in Asbury Park, New Jersey, used an ingenious ploy to engage her attention. On the back of the postcard, after asking her when she would return home, he wrote his initial signature in tremulous handwriting. He followed this with the postscript, "You see how nervous I am when thinking of you."

This postcard greeting seems to be an appropriate way to say THE END.

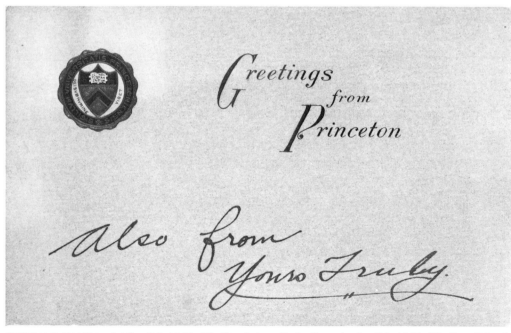

Publisher: Huston Engraving Co., Philadelphia, PA * Manufacturer: Huston Engraving Co., Philadelphia, PA * Type: Colored Engraving, Divided Back * Postmark: July 5, 1911 * Value Index: D

BIBLIOGRAPHY

Allmen, Diane, WHAT'S POSTCARD COLLECTING ALL ABOUT?, Wisconsin: Postcard Collector, 1984

Andrews, Barbara, A DIRECTORY OF POSTCARDS, ARTISTS, PUBLISHERS, AND TRADEMARKS, The Little Red Caboose, 1975

Barnes, James, A PRINCETONIAN, New York: G.P. Putnam's Sons, 1896

Bennett, Ira F. and others, THE NASSAU HERALD OF THE CLASS OF 1911, New Jersey: Princeton University Press, 1911

Bill, Alfred Hoyt, A HOUSE CALLED MORVEN, New Jersey: Princeton University Press, 1954

Blair, Roy and others, THE BENHAM CLUB OF PRINCETON, NEW JERSEY,

(Princeton) New Jersey: 1930

Breese, Gerald, PRINCETON UNIVERSITY LAND 1752—1984, New Jersey: Trustees of Princeton University, Princeton University Press, 1986

CAMPUS—A GUIDE TO PRINCETON UNIVERSITY, New Jersey: Office of Communications, Princeton, University, 1987

Carver, Sally S., THE AMERICAN POSTCARD GUIDE TO TUCK, Massachusetts: Carves Cards, 1976

Cawley, James and Margaret, ALONG THE DELAWARE AND RARITAN CANAL,

New Jersey: Associated University Press,Inc., 1970

Collins, Varnum Lansing, GUIDE TO PRINCETON—THE TOWN AND THE UNIVERSITY, New Jersey: Princeton University Press, 1920

Collins, Varnum Lansing, PRINCETON, New York: Oxford University Press, 1914

Collins, Varnum Lansing, PRINCETON PAST AND PRESENT, New Jersey: Princeton University Press, 1946

Corson, Walter E., edited by James L. Lowe, PUBLISHERS' TRADEMARKS IDENTIFIED, Pennsylvania: Deltiologists of America, 1979

Cottage Club, HISTORY OF THE UNIVERSITY COTTAGE CLUB OF PRINCETON, NEW JERSEY, (Princeton) New Jersey: Privately Printed, 1936

Craig, Robert W. and others, THE REPORT OF THE PRINCETON ARCHITECTURAL SURVEY, Prepared For the Joint Historic Sites Commission, (Princeton) New Jersey: 1981

DIAL, CANNON MERGE, Princeton Alumni Weekly Article, November 8, 1989

Egbert, Donald Drew, THE MODERN PRINCETON, New Jersey: Princeton University Press, 1947

Egbert, Donald Drew, PRINCETON PORTRAITS, New Jersey: Princeton University Press, 1947

Elliott, Len, ONE HUNDRED YEARS OF PRINCETON FOOTBALL, New Jersey: Princeton Athletic News, 1969

Elliot, Margaret Axson, MY AUNT LOUISA AND WOODROW WILSON, North Carolina: The University of North Carolina Press, 1944

Federal Writers Project, Works Progress Administration, OLD PRINCETON'S NEIGHBORS, New Jersey: The Graphic Arts Press, 1939

Fitzgeorge, Charles I, A FRAGMENTARY HISTORY OF THE METHODIST EPISCOPAL CHURCH OF PRINCETON, NEW JERSEY, Unpublished Typescript, 1933

Freeman, Larry, WISH YOU WERE HERE—A CENTENNIAL GUIDE TO POSTCARD COLLECTING, New York: Century House, Inc., 1976

THE GARGOYLES OF PRINCETON UNIVERSITY, New Jersey: Office of Communications/Publications, Princeton University,

Gibson, David and others, N.J. DELAWARE AND RARITAN CANAL STATE PARK—HISTORIC STRUCTURES SURVEY, Delaware and Raritan Canal Commission, 1982

Glas, Jonathan E. and others, TO PROVIDE PROTECTION, New Jersey:

Princeton Hook and Ladder 1788-1988, 1988

Greiff, Constance M., JOHN NOTMAN, ARCHITECT, Pennsylvania: The Athenaeum of Philadelphia, 1979

Greiff, Constance M. and others, PRINCETON ARCHITECTURE—A PICTORIAL HISTORY OF TOWN AND CAMPUS, New Jersey: Princeton University Press, 1967

Hageman, John F., HISTORY OF PRINCETON AND ITS INSTITUTIONS (2 Volumes), Pennyslvania: J.B. Lippincott & Company, 1879

HISTORIC PRINCETON, New Jersey: Princeton Municipal Improvement, Inc., 1940

Historical Society of Princeton, PRINCETON HISTORY, New Jersey:

Journal published periodically, Various issues

HISTORY OF THE IVY CLUB 1879-1929, New Jersey: 1929

Hobler, Randy and Jeanne Silvester, PRINCETON TRIVIA PERSPECTIVES, 1985

Holt, Tonie and Valmai, PICTURE POSTCARDS OF THE GOLDEN AGE,

Pennsylvania: Deltiologists of America, 1971

Klamkin, Marian, PICTURE POSTCARDS, New York: Dodd, Mead & Company, 1974

Lane, Wheaton J. PICTORIAL HISTORY OF PRINCETON UNIVERSITY, New Jersey: Princeton University Press, 1947

Leckie, Robert, FOOTBALL, New York: Random House, Inc., 1968

Leitch, Alexander, A PRINCETON COMPANION, New Jersey: Princeton University Press, 1978

Link, Arthur S. (Ed.), THE FIRST PRESBYTERIAN CHURCH OF PRINCETON, New Jersey: Princeton University Press, 1967

McKelvey, William J.Jr., THE DELAWARE & RARITAN CANAL—A PICTORIAL HISTORY, Pennsylvania: Canal Press Incorporated, 1975

Menzies, Elizabeth G.C., MILLSTONE VALLEY, New Jersey: Rutgers University Press, 1969

Menzies, Elizabeth G.C., PASSAGE BETWEEN RIVERS, New Jersey: Rutgers University Press, 1976

Morgan, Hal and Andreas Brown, PRAIRIE FIRES AND PAPER MOONS—THE AMERICAN PHOTOGRAPHIC POSTCARD: 1900-1920, Massachusetts: David R.Godine,Inc., 1981

Myers, William Starr and others, WOODROW WILSON—SOME PRINCETON MEMORIES, New Jersey: Princeton University Press, 1946

Nassau Presbyterian Church, HISTORICAL SKETCH OF NASSAU PRESBYTERIAN CHURCH, PRINCETON, NEW JERSEY, New Jersey: Booklet, 1986

Nevins, Allen, GROVER CLEVELAND—A STUDY IN COURAGE, New York: Dodd, Mead & Company, 1932

N.J. Dept. of Environmental Protection—Division of Park and Forestry,THE THOMAS CLARKE HOUSE, Pamphlet, 1986

Norris, Edwin Mark, THE STORY OF PRINCETON, Massachusetts: Little Brown, and Company, 1917

Osgood, Charles G., LIGHTS IN NASSAU HALL—A BOOK OF THE BICENTENNIAL-PRINCETON 1746—1946, New Jersey: Princeton University Press, 1951

Osgood, Charles G. and others, THE MODERN PRINCETON, New Jersey: Princeton University Press, 1947

Pinel, Stephen L., OLD ORGANS OF PRINCETON, New Hampshire: The Boston Organ Club Chapter of the Organ Historical Society, 1989

Presbrey, Frank and others, ATHLETICS AT PRINCETON, New York:

Frank Presbrey Company, 1901

(THE) PRINCETON BOOK, Massachusetts: Houghton, Osgood & Company, 1879

Princeton History Project, PRINCETON RECOLLECTOR, Various Issues

PRINCETON—PAST, PRESENT AND FUTURE, New Jersey: Princeton University Press, 1927

(THE) PRINCETON PACKET, New Jersey: Various issues

Range, Thomas E., THE BOOK OF POSTCARD COLLECTING, New York: E.P. Dutton, 1980

Reed, George Kinner, PALS OF MINE—CLASS OF NINETY-NINE—PRINCETON, Princeton, Class of 99', 1914

Ryan, Dorothy B., PICTURE POSTCARDS IN THE UNITED STATES 1893—1918, New York: Clarkson N. Potter, 1982

St. Paul Church, FROM HUMBLE BEGINNINGS 1843—1973, St. Paul Church, Princeton, New Jersey and St. James Mission Church, Rocky Hill, New Jersey, 1973

Saunders, Frances Wright, ELLEN AXSON WILSON—FIRST LADY BETWEEN TWO WORLDS, Chapel Hill, North Carolina: The University of North Carolina Press, 1985

Saunders, Frances Wright. PRINCETON HISTORY—THE WILSON YEARS, Unpublished audio tape, Princeton Adult School, 1986

Savage, Henry Lyttleton and others, NASSAU HALL 1756—1956.

New Jersey: Princeton University Press, 1956

Seeley G. Mudd Manuscript Library:

    File-Grounds and Buildings-Athletic Fields

    File-Grounds and Buildings-Class of 1887 Boat House

    File-Grounds and Buildings-Palmer Stadium

    File-Rowing

    Lowery, Charles F., AN ARCHITECTURAL ANALYSIS OF THE   PRINCETON UNIVERSITY EATING CLUBS 1905—1979, Manuscript.

    Myers, Richard Bruce, PROSPECT AVENUE AND THE EATING CLUBS   TO 1905, Manuscript.

Seldon, William K., THE LEGACY OF JOHN CLEVE GREEN, New Jersey: Office of Printing Services, Princeton University, 1988

Selden, William K., PRINCETON—THE BEST OLD PLACE OF ALL, New Jersey: Office of Printing Services, Princeton University, 1987

Snow, Richard, CONEY ISLAND—A POSTCARD JOURNEY TO THE CITY OF FIRE, New York: Brightwater Press, 1985

Steele, Valerie, FASHION AND EROTICISM—IDEAS OF FEMININE BEAUTY FROM VICTORIAN ERA TO THE JAZZ AGE, New York: Oxford University Press, 1985

Stillwell, Richard, THE CHAPEL OF PRINCETON UNIVERSITY, New Jersey: Princeton University Press, 1971

Tiger Inn, AN UNDERGRADUATE HISTORY OF THE TIGER INN, (Princeton) New Jersey: Privately published 1940

Tower Club, THE FIRST TWENTY-FIVE YEARS OF THE TOWER CLUB OF PRINCETON UNIVERSITY, New York: Braunworth & Co., Inc, 1928

TOWN TOPICS, (Princeton) New Jersey: Various issues

Ulyat, William L., THE PRINCETON DIRECTORY (FORMERLY STILLWELL'S PRINCETON DIRECTORY) 1910—1911, New Jersey: Compiled and Published by W. L. Ulyat

THE UNIVERSITY FIELD, New Jersey: The Daily Princetonian, September 26, 1892

Wallace, George R., PRINCETON SKETCHES, New York: G.P. Putnam's Sons, The Knickerbocker Press, 1893

Wertenbaker, Thomas Jefferson, PRINCETON 1746—1896, New Jersey: Princeton University Press, 1946

Williams, Jesse Lynch, PRINCETON STORIES, New York: Charles Scribner's Sons, 1895

Williams, John Rogers, THE HANDBOOK OF PRINCETON, New York: The Grafton Press, 1905

Wilmot, John R., THE PRINCETON BRANCH, Trains Magazine, June 1987

Index

Cover Design by Joe Arduini
Book design and layout by The Art Network
This book is set in 10.5 pointsBerkeley Medium, with 12 points of lead, with display type in Berkeley Bold.